REVOLUTIONARY INTERCOMMUNALISM
AND THE RIGHT OF NATIONS
TO SELF-DETERMINATION

REVOLUTIONARY INTERCOMMUNALISM

&

THE RIGHT OF NATIONS TO SELF-DETERMINATION

Huey P Newton

Vladimir Illych Lenin

Edited and introduced by Amy Gdala

First published as a Superscript paperback in 2004
by
Cyhoeddwyr y Superscript Ltd.,
404 Robin Square,
Newtown. Powys. Wales.

Cover design by Emma Jane Connolly from a photograph of the children of the Simon Napier Intercommunal Youth Institute.

ISBN 0954291344

Printed and bound by Antony Rowe, Eastbourne

Contents

"....for as we are never in a proper condition of doing justice to others, while we continue under the influence of some leading partiality, so neither are we capable of doing it to ourselves while we remain fettered by any obstinate prejudice."

Thomas Paine, *Common Sense*

Introduction

"Intercommunalism" has got itself a bad name. This is mainly because of the way the word (and its diminuitive "communalism") is used in the Indian subcontinent where the shared language of the old and new imperial powers has provided a shorthand term for the violence between religious or ethnic groups which those powers themselves kindled, and may even continue to inflame.

This shorthand use is particularly unfortunate because it can be argued - as I intend to do - that Huey P Newton's exposition of the concept of "Revolutionary Intercommunalism" is the most progressive, most logical and most hopeful political idea since Gandhi developed the principle of non-violent direct action.

The history of all hitherto existing culture is, of course, the history of the struggle between opposing sets of ideas, that is: between theses and their antitheses. Karl Marx took the first step towards a postmodern way of understanding the world when he characterised this as a war between classes, between haves and have-nots, between those who owned the land, and or capital, and those who had nothing to sell but themselves. Marx showed how the alienation from the essence of the human spirit that comes from the commodification, or dehumanisation, of labour demeans all the people - bourgeois and proletarian alike.

Marx was a brilliant sociologist but he was not a prophet. He could not foresee the trajectory of the rise of the joint stock company. Nor did he dream of a future time when stocks and shares would be so widely distributed that the Iron Lady (a.k.a the Robber Baroness) would "tell Sid" to "sell little pieces of himself by day" [CW Mills, 2000] to buy back tiny fractions of his own lost common treasury. He did not consider the complications of a time when the mass of the alienated and exploited people would find themselves straddling the property divide, one foot on each side, hopping on hot ashes, still wage-slaves but debt-slaves as well, people who, quite frankly, are of more value to "the economy" as **consumers** than they ever could be as **producers**.

It took the turn of a century and the mind of a thinker from a later age to realise the importance of the international dimension in consumer demand. It was V I Lenin who saw that, even though slavery had been theoretically abolished a generation back, capital would be increasingly invested across national boundaries, and labour exploited remotely. Where once Zola's miner or Tressell's urban artisan would salvage wood wherever he could, and knock together shelf , dresser or pot-cupboard in his few workfree hours, the cheap furniture that today's working man and his working wife can afford to buy new for themselves in IKEA was tooled the other side of the world.

But Lenin was no prophet either: he studied the Real Politik of International capital, but failed to anticipate the degree to which technological advance would accelerate the flow of labour, of capital, and of ideas.

Marx's theories were based on the gentile notions of bureaucracy that ruled the British Library, where the volumes he studied were reliably delivered to his green-leather-topped desk. Lenin's ideology was - despite its overtly international dimension - no less parochial, harking back, as it did, to the self-sacrificing certainties of Mother Russia (or Russian Mothers).

Again it would take another generation to produce the political theorist who could conceptualise the longer term impact of imperialism on the consciousness of humankind: the geographical dimension of relative deprivation, the rise of the supranational corporations and the globalisation of alienated desire. That theorist was Huey P Newton. His contribution was not so much in his elucidation of the new depths of injustice and exploitation existing in the so-called "post-colonial" period, as in his understanding that these conditions constituted the possibility of a higher level of ideological struggle that could lead to a means of greater enlightenment and fulfillment for all the peoples of the planet.

Huey himself was the youngest of seven children in a hardworking family, frequently moving around the San Francisco Bay area from one poor, segregated street to another. But he never felt deprived: he always had enough to eat, enjoyed the California climate, "which is kind to the poor", and thrived in the security of " a close family with a proud strong protective father and a loving, joyful mother." [HP Newton,1973, pp. 16,17]. School did its best one way and another to undermine his spirit but it did not succeed in this any more than it did in imparting basic literacy. At the age of sixteen Huey taught himself to read.

> I do not know how long it took me to go through Plato the first time, probably several months. When I finally finished, I started over again. I was not trying to deal with the ideas or concepts, just learning to recognize the words. I went through the book eight or nine times before I felt I had mastered the material. Later on, I studied *The Republic* in college. By then I was prepared for it. [Ibid, p.55].

But the discipline of Political Science was not "prepared for" Huey. The universities were not ready for his fresh and inspiring articulation of the principle of UNIVERSALISM, the principle which is at the heart of all the great philosophy from Plato through Plotinus and Aquinas to Kant.

Perhaps the easiest, though probably not the most

elegant, way of explaining UNIVERSALISM is to consider what it is **not**, what it is opposed to: to think about what it denies, and by denying, transcends.

According to Confucius, people's duty to each other is a function of closeness, whether genetic or preferential. So my greatest duty is to my closest relative or friend, and my obligation towards others decreases in direct proportion to my indifference to them. What Confucius is describing here is a principle of PARTICULARISM, the principle by which what we think and feel and do towards a person is seen as properly depending on precisely who that particular person is. Clearly the extreme conclusion of the advocacy of PARTICULARISM as a life strategy is the simple imperative to "Look after number one": yourself first and then the people closest to you. In this vein it is possible to read Spinoza's philosophy and Darwin's biological theory as though they generate an ethic of self-interest much like the one expounded in the glossy magazines: go on spoil yourself because you are worth it - you have a duty to pursue your own happiness.

On this reading the very best way to live is to look after yourself well, and you can show increased virtue by being nice to your family and friends. Your interaction with people is determined by their singularity, by **who** they are, not by what they are saying or playing, or building or destroying.

Self, family, tribe, and nation are to be honoured in

11

that order. This is the philosophy of autistic externalisation, conservatism, nationalism, nepotism, atavism. It is easy to see how little it would take in terms of cynical political manipulation to nudge the **indifference** that the PARTICULARIST culture feels towards outsiders into antipathy, antagonism, racism, violence - genocide.

The "strange fruit hanging on the Poplar tree" in the American deep South was a product of the seed of the principle of PARTICULARISM sowed generations earlier by the first truly global commercial operation since the Romans, where human beings were traded for cotton and sugar, traded as beasts of burden, as labour. They were not me or my close friends and family, you must understand, they were nothing to do with me. If I had been alive at the time, and I had known, I ought to have been indifferent to their plight because they were **nothing to do with me.**

In an admirable effort to remind us all of the logical consequences of that supreme indifference that is racism, modern Germany preserves, as museums, the sites of the gas chambers where the Nazis attempted to exterminate the entire 'races' of Slavs, gypsies and Jews. Yet nothing seems to have been learned. Indeed this holocaust has been invoked over and over again in attempts to plead other PARTICULARISTIC causes and justify other atrocities from the atomic bombs, that the victorious Allies dropped on Japan, to helicopter gun-ships that are mowing down civilians, even today, even as I write.

And this same day in Rwanda a slowly healing people attempts to give a final dignity to the victims of a genocide on just as unimaginable a scale.

'Race' against 'race', tribe against tribe, family against family, person against person, that is what PARTICULARISM means. And "all is fair in Love and War", there can be no rules because everybody is different, there is one rule for me and another for you, one for us and another for them. That is what PARTICULARISM is. It is the law of the jungle, where "might is right" (or at least justifiable in terms of something called "evolutionary psychology") and one's first duty is personal survival.

Within the PARTICULARIST culture the only way to keep order is by the imposition of a Leviathan, a nepotistic, hierarchical apparatus of state, with armies, police, Witchfinder Generals, Secret Services, Social Services and Mental Health legislation.[Hobbes, 1998; Kai T Erikson, 1968; Todd and Fitzgerald, 2003; Box, 1971; Foucault, 2001] Such covertly authoritarian regimes are sometimes theocratic, and (though some of their commanders may be female like Eva Peron, Golda Meyer, Margaret Thatcher and Eugenia Charles) they are usually patriarchal.

The teenage political theorist Newton understood the connection between patriarchy and PARTICULARISM even before he started on Plato.

13

I had such respect and admiration for my father that I could not openly question his life. He would not have understood what I was going through. I was grateful, I was appreciative, and I loved and admired him, but I had questions not easily answered.

It was the beatnik era in the Bay area , and I grew a beard. To my parents, a beard meant a bohemian, and my father insisted that I shave it off. I refused. Because he was accustomed to wielding total authority in our family, my refusal was a serious family violation. My father pressed me again to shave; I continued to resist. The climax came abruptly one night when he confronted me with an ultimatum to shave right then and there. I told him I would not do it. He struck me, and I ran to him , grabbing him with a bear hug to restrain his arms and then pushing him away. He chased me out of the house, but I could run much faster. I also knew that I was strong enough to overpower him, but I would never have done that. I just fled.[Ibid p. 59]

The sweet irony is that it was the very loving nature of his close and caring family that gave the young Huey the personal and spiritual strength to conceive of a kind of love that transcends the particular and renders it irrelevant. He called it Revolutionary Love.

Revolutionary Love is not the kind of romantic fiction that aspires to "living happily ever after behind a white picket fence" [Ibid, p.96]. Rather it is the practice of the philosophy of

Immanuel Kant.

Kant had two basic points to make, neither of them actually new, both of them vital to the development of the perspective of UNIVERSALISM.

First Kant stressed the importance of distinguishing between **phenomena** (happenings and things) and **nuomena** (ideas or modes of understanding). Huey Newton was impressed with the application of this distinction in the work of the twentieth century Logical Positivists.

> These ideas have helped me to develop my own thinking and ideology. Ayer once stated, "Nothing can be real if it cannot be conceptualized, articulated and shared." That notion stuck with me and became very important when I began to use the ideological method of dialectical materialism as a world view. The ideology of the Black Panthers stands on that premise and proceeds on that basis...[Ibid p 68]

Kant's second contribution to the systematic conceptualisation of UNIVERSALISM lies in his explication of the **categorical imperative.**

My own grandmother (Amelia Noble) was an exact contemporary of Huey's (Estella O'Neal). A portrait of his reminds me of mine - the physique, the hair style, the body language and the cut of the cloth. I wonder if the similarity

15

extended to the simple "What-if-everybody-did-it?" morality that mine drummed into me. If I dropped a sweet paper she would demand that I pick it up.

"But it's only a small sweet paper what harm is it doing?"

"What if everybody did it? The whole world would be knee-deep in litter."

Kant's famous imperative requires each of us to act as though we were 'Universal Legislators'. He asks us to consider the consequences of turning our actions into a rule that everyone else would have to follow. Would the world be a better place if everybody acted like us? Or would it be knee-deep in crap?

Newton's notion of revolution is entirely Kantian, entirely UNIVERSALISTIC. There is no idea of revenge or retribution in the revolutionary struggle, no descent to the barbarism or tribalism of vendetta. The Categorical Imperative - known for generations before Kant as the 'Golden Rule' - forbids one to do anything to anyone else that one would not wish done to oneself. This is an idea of staggering profundity championed by educators as venerated as the Prophet Jesus and Archbishop Tutu.

True revolutionary justice has nothing to do with

vengeance. If I have acted badly towards another person I would want them to admonish me, not with bitterness and self-righteous anger, but with loving regard for my own understanding and development. This way there is hope that I will learn from the experience. This is to turn the other cheek but not a blind eye. It is to educate and improve the transgressors rather than to "teach them a lesson" in the sense that the Palestinians are supposed to be "taught a lesson" by having their homes bulldozed into the ground and their crippled clerics "taken out" with "surgically" precise missiles.

In South Africa this ideal of restitutive rather than retributive justice has been the foundation not only for the Truth and Reconciliation Commission, but for the constitution itself.

And in Rwanda (where the perpetrators of the genocide were Christian Hutus, and those who had the courage to extend love across the 'tribal/racial' divide were mainly Muslims and atheists) the healing process is begun by a national policy of transtribal adoption for the countless orphans, and an NGO-inspired symbolic exchange of cattle where every calf born to a Tutsi-owned cow is given to a Hutu family and *vice versa*.

Christianity, like every other ideology or religion, is open to misinterpretation and exploitation by ruthless patriarchs and power mongers. But it is no mere coincidence that when Newton struggles to account for the origins of his own nuomenal landscape - in addition to writers as varied as "Watson ... Skinner and Pavlov...Camus, Sartre, Kierkegaard... Mao Tse Tung ...(and) Malcolm X" [Ibid pp.68-71] - he is always falling back on The Bible. For Christianity itself provides a close parallel to Newton's concept of Revolutionary Intercommunalism. It is a set of universalistic principles universally (if hypocritically) proclaimed by imperial powers to all the diverse communities of the imperialised.

In what Newton described as the 'existentialism' of the Book of Ecclesiastes, and in the Sermon on the Mount, the imperial victims found the intellectual weapons (as well as the spiritual strength) to face their oppressors. No coincidence either, then, that the rhythm and harmonies of Gospel music provided the template for the revolutionary battle hymns.

Yet Christianity is neither necessary nor sufficient for the development of the kind of ideas actualised in the South African constitution. A secular formulation of UNIVERSAL-ISM could have done the job just as well. But, of course the imperial boot did not imprint the sparse logic of Immanuel Kant, simply because there was nothing in it for Empire - Christianity is more easily mystified and magicalised. And, like most religions, it is readily permissive of the institutions of theocracy, hierarchy and patriarchy which negate the essence of its UNIVERSALISM with the kind of atavistic PARTICUL-

18

ARISM that is of such value to the builders of empires and the bringers of global exploitation and destruction.

Add to this the idea of waiting until we get to Heaven to know what happiness is, and the value of Christianity to Empire is clear.

Huey says,

> Sometimes I got into teaching on the block, reciting poetry or starting dialogues about philosophical ideas. I talked to the brothers about things that Hume, Pierce, Locke or William James had said, and in that way I retained ideas and sometimes resolved problems in my own mind.
>
> ...we talked about such questions as the existence of God, self-determination, and free-will. I would ask them, "Do you have free will?"
> "Yes."
> "Do you believe in God?"
> "Yes."
> "Is your God all-powerful?"
> "Yes."
> "Is he omniscient?"
> "Yes."
>
> Therefore, I told them, their all-powerful God knew everything before it happened. If so, I would ask, "How can you say you have free will when He knows what you are going to do before you do it? You are predestined to do what you do. If not, then your God has lied or He has made a mistake, and you have already said that your God cannot lie or make a mistake." These dilemmas led to arguments that

19

lasted all day, over a fifth of wine though I sometimes went to school drunk.[Newton, 1973, p.75]

Dialectical materialism is never about final solutions. Ideological dilemmas do not bring understanding through lazy quests for quick resolution or 'closure'. Newton's dialogues on intercommunalism are the quintessence of permanent revolution on the nuomenal plane. They beckon us to a struggle without end, a struggle without which our little lives would be wasted in the harsh turn-up-for-the-book that innocent fools will end up calling 'History', and cynical operators will label "The End of History" [Fukuyama,1993].

In this book the transcripts of Newton's statements and discussions in the Spring of 1971 are set beside V I Lenin's argument with Rosa Luxemburg on the same subject half a century earlier. It is for the reader to assess the value of these perspectives now that

> "the declining autonomy of nation states and the rise of shifting non-state coalitions have provided a new terrain of opportunity not only for the disaffected but also for opportunist use and sponsorship of terrorism by states themselves" [Todd and Bloch, 2003].

Intercommunalism

In early February 1971 a group of social theorists met at Yale. They sat around a huge mahogany table in the library of Trumbull College: fourteen students (Alan Beller, Samuel Cooper, John Cole, William Horowitz, Sandra Hughes, Caroline Jackson, Vera Jones, Ann Linden, Jennifer Lyman, Donald Mendelsohn, Wayne Neveu, Dwight Raiford, Kurt Schmoke and Bradley Wong), two academic socologists in the role of moderators, an elderly psychoanalyic theorist (Erik H Erikson) and Huey P Newton, Supreme Commander of the Black Panther Party.

As Kai T Erikson, one of the moderators, recorded,

> ...an equal number of onlookers formed another circle outside them - behind Newton, a half-ring of comrades and travel companions, and behind Erikson, in awkward symmetry, a half-ring of Yale people. Without any conscious intent , the stage had been set for a confrontation. [K T Erikson, in E H Erikson and H P Newton, 1973, p7].

Confrontation was the keynote of the time, this was the season of the shootings at Jackson State and Kent State universities, and of the Panther Trials.

The dialogue began with a statement from Newton.

21

I'll start the discussion by explaining the Black Panther Party's ideology.

We believe that everything is in a constant state of change, so we employ a framework of thinking that can put us in touch with the process of change. That is, we believe that the conclusions will always change, but the fundamentals of the method by which we arrive at our conclusions will remain constant. Our ideology therefore, is the most important part of our thinking.

There are many different ideologies or schools of thought, and all of them start with an *a priori* set of assumptions. This is because mankind is still limited in its knowledge and finds it hard, at this historical stage, to talk about the very beginning of things and the very end of things without starting from premises that cannot yet be proved.

This is true of both general schools of thought— the idealist and the materialist. The idealists base their thinking on certain presumptions about things of which they have very little knowledge; the materialists like to believe that they are very much in contact with reality, or the real material world, disregarding the fact that they only assume there *is* a material world.

The Black Panther Party has chosen materialist assumptions on which to ground its ideology. This is a purely arbitrary choice. Idealism might be the real happening; we might not be here at all. We don't know whether we are in Connecticut or in San Francisco, whether we are dreaming and in a dream state, or whether we are awake and in a dream state. Perhaps we are just somewhere in a void; we simply can't be sure. But because the members of the Black Panther Party are materialists, we believe that some day scientists will be able to deliver the information that will give us not only the evidence but the proof that there is a material world and that its genesis was material—motion and matter—not spiritual.

Until that time, however, and for the purposes of this discussion, I merely ask that we agree on the stipulation that a material world exists and develops externally and independently of us all. With this stipulation, we have the foundation for an intelligent dialogue. We **assume** that there is a material world and that it exists and develops independently of us; and we assume that the human organism, through its sensory system, has the ability to observe and analyze that material world.

Now the dialectical materialist believes that everything in existence has fundamental internal contradictions. For example, the African gods south of the Sahara always had at least two heads, one for evil and one for good. Now people create God in their own image, what they think He—for God is always a "He" in patriarchal societies—what He is like or should be. So the African said, in effect: I am both good and evil; good and evil are the two parts of the thing that is me.
This is an example of an internal contradiction.

Western societies, though, split up good and evil, placing God up in heaven and the Devil down in hell. Good and evil fight for control over people in Western religions, but

23

they are two entirely different entities. This is an example of an external contradiction.

This struggle of mutually exclusive opposing tendencies within everything that exists explains the observable fact that all things have motion and are in a constant state of transformation. Things transform themselves because while one tendency or force is more dominating than another, change is nonetheless a constant, and at some point the balance will alter and there will be a new qualitative development. New properties will come into existence, qualities that did not altogether exist before. Such qualities cannot be analysed without understanding the forces struggling within the object in the first place, yet the limitations and determinations of these new qualities are not defined by the forces that created them.

Class conflict develops by the same principles that govern all other phenomena in the material world. In contemporary society, a class that owns property dominates a class that does not own property. There is a class of workers and a class of owners, and because there exists a basic contradiction in the interests of those two classes, they are constantly struggling with one another. Now, because things do not stay the same we can be sure of one thing: the owner will not stay the owner, and the people who are dominated will not stay dominated. We don't know exactly how this will happen, but after we analyze all the other elements of the situation, we can make a few predictions. We can be sure that if we increase the intensity of the struggle, we will reach a point where the equilibrium of forces will change and there will be a qualitative leap into a new situation with a new social equilibrium. I say "leap" because we know from our experience of the physical world that when transformations of this kind occur they do so with great force.

These principles of dialectical development do not represent an iron law that can be applied mechanically to the social process. There are exceptions to those laws of development and transformation, which is why, as dialectical materialists, we emphasize that we must analyze each set of conditions separately and make concrete analyses of concrete conditions in each instance. One cannot always predict the outcome, but one can for the most part gain enough insight to manage the process.

The dialectical method is essentially an ideology, yet we believe that it is superior to other ideologies because it puts us more in contact with what we believe to be the real world; it increases our ability to deal with that world and shape its development and change.

You could easily say, "Well, this method may be successfully applied in one particular instance, but how do you know that it is an infallible guide in all cases?" The answer is that we don't know. We don't say "all cases" or "infallible guide" because we try not to speak in such absolute and inclusive terms. We only we have to say that we have to analyze each instance, that we have found this method the best available in the course of our analyses, and that we think the method will continue to prove itself in the future.

We sometimes have a problem because people do not understand the ideology that Marx and Engels began to develop. People say, "You claim to be Marxists, but did you know that Marx was a racist?" We say, "Well, he probably was a racist: he made a statement once about the marriage of a white woman and a black man, and he called the black man a gorilla or something like that." The Marxists claim he was only kidding and that the statement shows Marx's closeness to the man, but of course that is nonsense. So it does seem that Marx was a racist.

Now if you are a **Marxist**, then Marx's racism affects your own judgment because a Marxist is someone who worships Marx and the thought of Marx. Remember, though, that Marx himself said, "I am not a Marxist." Such Marxists cherish the conclusions which Marx arrived at through his method, but they throw away the method itself—leaving themselves in a totally static posture. That is why most Marxists really are historical materialists: they look to the past to get answers for the future, and that does not work.

If you are a **dialectical materialist**, however, Marx's racism does not matter. You do not believe in the conclusions of one person but in the validity of a mode of thought; and we in the Party, as dialectical materialists, recognize Karl Marx as one of the great contributors to that mode of thought. Whether or not Marx was a racist is irrelevant and immaterial to whether or not the system of thinking he helped develop delivers truths about processes in the material world. And this is true in all disciplines. In every discipline you find people who have distorted visions and are at a low state of consciousness who nonetheless have flashes of insight and produce ideas worth considering. For instance, John B. Watson once stated that his favorite pastime was hunting and hanging niggers, yet he made great forward strides in the analysis and investigation of conditioned responses.

Now that I have said a word about the ideology of the Party, I am going to describe the history of the Party and how we have changed our understanding of the world.

When we started in October 1966, we were what one would call Black Nationalists. We realized the contradictions in society, the pressure on Black people in particular, and we saw that most people in the past had solved some of their problems by forming into nations. We therefore argued that it was rational and logical for us to believe that our sufferings as a people would end when we established a nation of our own, composed of our own people.

But after a while we saw that something was wrong with this resolution of the problem. In the past, nationhood was a fairly easy thing to accomplish. If we look around now, though, we see that the world—the land space, the livable parts as we know them—is pretty well settled. So we realized that to create a new nation we would have to become a dominant faction in this one, and yet the fact that we did not have power was the contradiction that drove us to seek nationhood in the first place. It is an endless circle you see: to achieve nationhood, we needed to become a dominant force; but to become a dominant force we needed to be a nation.

So we made a further analysis and found that in order for us to be a dominant force we would at least have to be great in number. So we developed from just plain nationalists or separatist nationalists into revolutionary nationalists. We said

27

that we joined with all of the other people in the world struggling for decolonialization and nationhood, and called ourselves a "dispersed colony" because we did not have the geographical concentration that other so-called colonies had. But we did have Black communities throughout the country — San Francisco, Los Angeles, New Haven — and there are many similarities between these communities and the traditional kind of colony. We also thought that if we allied with those other colonies we would have a greater number, a greater chance, a greater force; and that is what we needed, of course, because only force kept us a colonized people.

We saw that it was not only beneficial for us to be revolutionary nationalists but to express our solidarity with those friends who suffered many of the same kind of pressures we suffered. Therefore we changed our self-definitions. We said that we are not only revolutionary nationalists — that is, nationalists who want revolutionary changes in everything, including the economic system the oppressor inflicts upon us — but we are also individuals deeply concerned with the other people of the world and their desires for revolution. In order to show this solidarity, we decided to call ourselves internationalists.

Originally, as I said, we assumed that people could solve a number of their problems by becoming nations, but this conclusion showed our lack of understanding of the world's dialectical development. Our mistake was to assume that the conditions under which people had become nations in the past still existed. To be a nation, one must satisfy certain essential conditions, and if these things do not exist or cannot be created, then it is not possible to be a nation.

In the past, nation-states were usually inhabited by people of a certain ethnic and religious background. They were divided from other people either by a partition of water or a great unoccupied land space. This natural partition gave the nation's dominant class, and the people generally, a certain amount of control over the kinds of political, economic, and social institutions they established. It gave them a certain control over their destiny and their territory. They were secure at least to the extent that they would not be attacked or violated by another nation ten thousand miles away, simply because the means to transport troops that far did not exist. This situation, however, could not last. Technology developed until there was a definite qualitative transformation in the relationships within and between nations.

We know that you cannot change a part of the whole without changing the whole, and vice versa. As technology developed and there was an increase in military capabilities and means of travel and communication, nations began to control other territories, distant from their own. Usually they controlled these other lands by sending administrators and settlers, who would extract labor from the people or resources from the earth - or both. This is the phenomenon we colonialism.

The settlers' control over the seized land and people grew to such an extent that it wasn't even necessary for the settler to be present to maintain the system. He went back home. The people were so integrated with the aggressor that their land didn't look like a colony any longer. But because their land didn't look like a free state either, some theorists started to call these lands "neocolonies." Arguments about the precise definition of these entities developed. Are they colonies or not? If they aren't, what are they? The theorists knew that something had happened, but they did not know what it was.

Using the dialectical materialist method, we in the Black Panther Party saw that the United States was no longer a nation. It was something else; it was more than a nation. It had not only expanded its territorial boundaries, but it had expanded all of its controls as well. We called it an empire. Now at one time the world had an empire in which the conditions of rule were different—the Roman Empire. The difference between the Roman and the American empires is that other nations were able to exist external to and independent of the Roman Empire because their means of exploration, conquest, and control were all relatively limited.

But when we say "empire" today, we mean precisely what we say. An empire is a nation-state that has transformed itself into a power controlling **all** the lands and people.

We believe that there are no more colonies or neo-**colonies**. If a people is colonized, it must be possible for them to decolonize and become what they formerly were. But what happens when the raw materials are extracted and labor is exploited within a territory dispersed over the entire globe? When the riches of the whole earth are depleted and used to feed a gigantic industrial machine in the imperialist's home? Then the people and the economy are so integrated into the imperialist empire that it's impossible to "decolonize", to return to the former conditions of existence.

If colonies cannot decolonize and return to their

30

original existence as nations, then nations no longer exist. Nor, we believe, will they ever exist again. And since there must be nations for revolutionary nationalism or internationalism to make sense, we decided that we would have to call ourselves something new.

We **say** that the world today is a dispersed collection of communities. A community is different from a nation. A community is a small unit with a comprehensive collection of institutions that exist to serve a small group of people. And we say further that the struggle in the world today is between the small circle that administers and profits from the empire of the United States, and the peoples of the world who want to determine their own destinies.

We call this situation intercommunalism. We are now in the age of reactionary intercommunalism, in which a ruling circle, a small group of people, control all other people by using their technology.

At the same time, we say that this technology can solve most of the material contradictions people face, that the material conditions exist that would allow the people of the world to develop a culture that is essentially human and would nurture those things that would allow the people to resolve contradictions in a way that would not cause the mutual slaughter of all of us. The development of such a culture would be revolutionary intercommunalism.

Some communities have begun doing this. They liberated their territories and have established provisional governments. We recognize them, and say that these governments represent the people of China, North Korea, the

31

people in the liberated zones of South Vietnam, and the people in North Vietnam. We believe their examples should be followed so that the order of the day would not be reactionary intercommunalism (empire) but revolutionary intercommunalism. The people of the world, that is, must seize power from the small ruling circle and expropriate the expropriators, pull them down from their pinnacle and make them equals, and distribute the fruits of our labor, that have been denied us, in some equitable way. We know that the machinery to accomplish these tasks exists and we want access to it.

Imperialism has laid the foundation for world communism, and imperialism itself has grown to the point of reactionary intercommunalism because the world is now integrated into one community. The communications revolution, combined with the expansive domination of the American empire, has created the "global village." The peoples of all cultures are under siege by the same forces and they all have access to the same technologies.

There are only differences in degree between what's happening to the Blacks here and what's happening to all of the people in the world, including Africans. Their needs are the same and their energy is the same. And the contradictions they suffer will only be resolved when the people establish a revolutionary intercommunalism where they share all the wealth that they produce and live in one world.

The stage of history is set for such a transformation: the technological and administrative base of socialism exists. When the people seize the means of production and all social institutions, then there will be a qualitative leap and a change in the organization of society. It will take time to resolve the contradictions of racism and all kinds of chauvinism; but because the people will control their own social institutions, they will be free to re-create themselves and to establish communism, a stage of human development in which human values will shape the structures of society. At this time the world will be ready for a still higher level, of which we can now know nothing.

Dialectics

When Newton finished his statement there followed a question and answer session which was recorded on audio tape and subsequently transcribed. Unfortunately the list of names to accompany the tape was mislaid, so the questioners cannot be identified individually.

QUESTION: I'm wondering: now that you have established an ideology with which to view the kinds of imperialism going on in the United States, what do you do once the revolution has taken place? What happens once you have taken over the structures made by capitalism and have assumed responsibility for them? Aren't you going to encounter the same struggles between the dominant forms of government and the inferior?

NEWTON: It's not going to be the same because nothing remains the same. All things are in a constant state of transformation, and therefore you will have other contradictions inherent in that new phenomenon. We can be very sure that there will be contradictions after revolutionary intercommunalism is the order of the day, and we can even be sure that there will be contradictions after communism, which is an even higher stage than revolutionary intercommunalism. There will always be contradictions or else everything would stop. So it's not a question of "when the revolution comes": the revolution is always going on. It is not a question of "when the revolution is going to be": revolution is going on every day, every minute, because the new is always struggling against the old for dominance.

We also say that every determination is a limitation, and every limitation is a determination. This is the struggle of the old and new again, where a thing seems to negate itself. For instance, imperialism negates itself after laying the foundation for communism, and communism will eventually negate itself because of its internal contradictions, and then we'll move to an even higher state. I like to think that we will finally move to a stage called "godliness," where man will know the secrets of the beginning and the end and will have full control of the universe - and when I say the universe, I mean all motion and matter.. This is only speculation, of course, because science has not delivered us the answer yet; but we believe that it will in the future.

So of course there will be contradictions in the future. But some contradictions are antagonistic and some contradictions are not antagonistic. Usually when we speak of antagonistic contradictions, we are talking about contradictions that develop from conflicts of economic interest, and we assume that in the future, when the people have power, these antagonistic contradictions will occur less and less.

QUESTION: Could you speak to the question of how you are going to expropriate the expropriators when they are the ones with the army and the ones with the police force?

NEWTON: Well, all things carry a negative sign as well as a positive sign. That's why we say every determination has a limitation and every limitation has a determination. For example, your organism carries internal contradictions from the moment you are born and begin to deteriorate. First you are an infant, then a small child, then an adolescent, and so on until you are old. We keep developing and burning ourselves out at the same time; we are negating ourselves. And this is just how imperialism is negating itself now. It's moved into a phase we call reactionary intercommunalism and has thus laid the foundation for revolutionary intercommunalism, because as the enemy disperses its troops and controls more and more space, it becomes weaker and weaker, you see. And as they become weaker and weaker, the people become stronger and stronger.

QUESTION: You spoke of technological differences between the various countries of the world. How are you going to integrate all these countries into intercommunalism if these differences exist?

NEWTON: They are already integrated by the mere fact that the ruling circle has control of all of them. Inside the geographical region of North America, for example, you have Wall Street, you have the big plants in Detroit turning out automobiles, and you have Mississippi, where there are no automobile factories. Does that mean that Mississippi is not a part of the complete whole? No, it only means that the expropriators have chosen to put automobile plants in Detroit rather than in Mississippi. Instead of producing automobiles, they grow food in Mississippi that makes stronger the hands of people in Detroit or Wall Street. So the answer to your question is that systems are inclusive: just because you don't have a factory in every single community does not mean that the community is distinct and independent and autonomous, you see.

QUESTION: Well, then, do you see each of the dispersed communities having certain kinds of things to work

36

out among themselves before they can take part in intercommunalism?

NEWTON: They **are** part of intercommunalism, reactionary intercommunalism. What the people have to do is become conscious of this condition. The primary concern of the Black Panther Party is to lift the level of consciousness of the people through theory and practice to the point where they will see exactly what is controlling them and what is oppressing them, and therefore see exactly what has to be done – or at least what the first step is. One of the greatest contributions of Freud was to make people aware that they are controlled much of their lives by their unconscious. He attempted to strip away the veil from from the unconscious and make it conscious: that's the first step in feeling free, the first step in exerting control. It seems to be natural for people not to like being controlled. Marx made a similar contribution to human freedom, only he pointed out the **external** things that control people. In order for people to liberate themselves from external controls, they have to know about these controls. Consciousness of the expropriator is necessary for expropriating the expropriator, for throwing off external controls.

QUESTION: So, in the ultimate intercommune, do you see separate, geographically defined communities that have had a specific history and a unique set of experiences? I mean, would each community retain some kind of separate identity?

NEWTON: No, I think that whether we like it or not, dialectics would make it necessary to have a universal identity. If we do not have universal identity, then we will have cultural, racial, and religious chauvinism, the kind of ethnocentrism we have now. So we say that even if in the future there will be some small differences in behavior patterns, different environments would all be a secondary thing. And we struggle for a future in which we will realize that we are all Homo sapiens and have more in common than not. We will be closer together than we are now.

QUESTION: I would like to return to something we were talking about a minute or two ago. It seems to me that the mass media have, in a sense, psychologized many of the people in our country, our own geographical area, so that they come to **desire** the controls that are imposed upon them by the capitalist system. So how are we going to fight this revolution if a great number of people, in this country at least, are in fact psychologically part of the ruling class?

NEWTON: Part of or controlled by?

QUESTION: Well, part of in the psychological sense, because they are not really in power. It's a psychological way of talking about the middle class. Do you have any feelings on that?

NEWTON: First, we have to understand that everything has a material basis, and that our personalities would not exist, what others call our spirit or our mind would not exist, if we were not material organisms. So to understand why some of the victims of the ruling class might identify with the ruling circle, we must look at their material lives; and if we do, we will realize that the same people who identify with the ruling circle are also very unhappy. Their feelings can be compared to those of a child: a child desires to mature so that he can control himself, but he believes he needs the protection of his father to do so. He has conflicting drives. Psychologists

38

would call this conflict neurotic if the child were unable to resolve it.

In a sense, then, that is what we are all about. First, people have to be conscious of the ways they are controlled, then we have to understand the scientific laws involved, and once that is accomplished, we can begin to do what we want—to manipulate phenomena.

QUESTION: But if the opposing forces at this point include a very large number of people, including most of the middle classes, then where will the revolutionary thrust come from?

NEWTON: O.K., I see what you are getting at. That thrust will come from the growing number of what we call "unemployables" in this society. We call Blacks and third world people in particular, and poor people in general, "unemployables" because they do not have the skills needed to work in a highly developed technological society. You remember my saying that every society, like every age, contains its opposites: feudalism produced capitalism, which wiped out feudalism, and capitalism produced socialism, which will wipe out capitalism. Now the same is true of reactionary intercommunalism. Technological development creates a large middle class, and the number of workers increases also. The workers are paid a good deal and get many comforts. But the ruling class is still only interested in itself. They might make certain compromises and give a little—as a matter of fact,the ruling circle has even developed something of a social structure or welfare state to keep the opposition down—but as technology develops, the need decreases. It has been estimated that ten years from now only a small percentage of the present work force will be necessary to run the industries. Then what will happen to your worker who is now making four dollars an hour? The working class will be narrowed down, the class of unemployables will grow because it will take more and more skills to operate those machines and fewer people. And as these people become unemployables, they will become more and more alienated; even socialist compromises will not be enough. You will then find an integration between, say, the Black unemployable and the white racist hard-hat who is not regularly employed and is mad at the Blacks who he thinks threaten his job. We hope that he will join forces with those people who are already unemployable, but whether he does or not, his material existence will have changed. The proletarian will become the lumpen proletarian. It is this future change—the increase of the lumpen proletariat and the decrease of the proletariat—which makes us say that the lumpen proletariat is the majority and carries the revolutionary banner.

QUESTION: I'd like to ask you a question about the Party. You said that you see the Black Panther Party as primarily a force to educate people, raise their consciousness, end their oppression, and so on. Do you see the Party as educating Black people specifically or as educating everybody?

NEWTON: We say that Black people are the vanguard of the revolution in this country, and, since no one will be free until the people of America are free, that Black people are the vanguard of world revolution. We don't say this in a boasting way. We inherit this legacy primarily because we are the last, you see, and as the saying goes, "The last will be the first".

We believe that Black Americans are the first real

internationalists; not just the Black Panther Party, but Black people who live in America. We are internationalists because we have been internationally dispersed by slavery, and we can easily identify with other people in other cultures. Because of slavery, we never really felt attached to the nation in the same way that the peasant was attached to the soil in Russia. We are always a long way from home.

And, finally the historical condition of Black Americans has led us to be progressive. We've always talked equality, you see, instead of believing that other people must equal us. What we want is not dominance, but for the yoke to be released. We want to live with other people, we don't want to say that we are better: in fact, if we suffer a fault, it is that we tend to feel we are worse than other people because we have been brainwashed to think that way. So these subjective factors, based on the material existence of Black people in America, contribute to our vanguard position.

Now as far as the Party is concerned, it has been exclusively Black so far. We are thinking about how to deal with the racist situation in America and the reaction Black people in America have to racism. We have to get to the Black people first because they were carrying the banner first, and we try to do everything possible to get them to relate to us.

QUESTION: You were saying something a while ago about the problem of simplifying your ideology for the masses. Could you say a little more about it?

NEWTON: Yes, that's our big burden. So far I haven't been able to do it well enough to keep from being booed off the stage, but we are learning. I think one way to show how

41

dialectics works is to use practical example after practical example. The reason I am sometimes afraid to do that is that people will take each example and think, "Well, if this is true in one case then it must be true in all other cases." If they do that, then they become historical materialists like most Marxist scholars and most Marxist parties. These scholars and parties don't really deal in dialectics at all, or else they would know that at this time the revolutionary banner will not be carried by the proletarian class but by the lumpen proletariat.

QUESTION: Talking about contradictions, one of the most obvious contradictions within the Black community is the difference in outlook between the Black bourgeoisie and the Black lower class. How do you raise the level of consciousness in the community to the point where the Black bourgeoisie sees its own intersts as being the same as those of the lower class?

NEWTON: Well, we are again dealing with attitudes and values that have to be changed. The whole concept of the bourgeoisie—Black bourgeoisie—is something of an illusion. It's a fantasy bourgeoisie, and this is true of most of the white bourgeoisie too. There are very few controllers even in the white middle class. They can barely keep their heads above water, they are paying all the bills, living hand-to-mouth, and they have the extra expense of refusing to live like Black people, you see. So they are not really controlling anything: they are controlled.

In the same way, I don't recognize the Black bourgeoisie as different from any other exploited people. They are living in a fantasy world, and the main thing is to instill consciousness, to point out their real interests, their objective and true interests, just as our white progressive and radical friends have to do in the white community.

QUESTION: How do you go about raising the level of consciousness in the Black community? Educationally, I mean. Do you have formal programs of instruction?

NEWTON: Well, we saw a need to formalize education because we didn't believe that a haphazard kind of learning would necessarily bring about the best results. We also saw that the so-called halls of learning did nothing but miseducate us; they either drove us out or kicked us out. They did me both ways. So what we are trying to do is structure an educational institution of our own.

Our first attempt along these lines is what we call our Ideological Institute. So far we have about fifty students, and these fifty students are — well, may I say unique students, because all of them are brothers and sisters off the block. What I mean is that they are lumpen proletarians. Most of them are kick-outs and dropouts; most of them left school in the eighth, ninth, or tenth grade. And those few who stayed all the way didn't learn how to read or write, just as I didn't learn until I was about sixteen. But now they are dealing with dialectics and they are dealing with science—they study physics and mathematics so that they can understand the universe—and they are learning because they think it is relevant to them now. They will relate this learning back to the community and the community will in turn see the need for our program. It's very practical and relates to the needs of the people in a way that makes them receptive to our teachings and helps open their eyes to the fact that the people are the real power. They are the ones who will bring about change, not us alone. A vanguard is like the head of a spear, the thing that goes first. But what really hurts is the butt of the spear, because even though the head makes the necessary entrance, the back part is what penetrates. Without the butt, a spear is nothing but a toothpick.

QUESTION:What about Malcolm X University? Would you say that it has value?

NEWTON: The whole issue is: who controls? We, the Black Panther Party, control our Ideological Institute. If the people (and when I say "the people" I mean the oppressed people) control Malcolm X University, if they control it without reservation or without having to answer for what is done there or who speaks there, then Malcolm X University is progressive. If that is not the case, then Malcolm X University, or any university by any other name, is not progressive. I like its name, though. [laughter]

QUESTION: The thing I don't understand is: if unity of identity is going to exist in revolutionary intercommunalism, then what will be the contradictions that produce further change? Like, it seems to me that it would be virtually impossible to avoid some contradictions.

NEWTON: I agree with you. You cannot avoid contradictions, you cannot avoid the struggle of opposite tendencies within the same wholes. But I can't tell you what the new opposites will be because they are not in existence yet. See what I mean?

QUESTION: I guess so. But how does all that fit in with your idea of a unified identity?

NEWTON: Well, in the first place, we do not deal in

panaceas. The qualitative leap from reactionary intercommunalism to revolutionary intercommunalism will not be the millennium. It will not immediately bring into being either a universal identity or a culture that is essentially human. It will only provide the material base for the development of those tendencies.

When the people seize the means of production,when they seize the mass media and so forth, you will still have racism, you will still have ethnocentrism, you will still have contradictions. But the fact that the people will be in control of all the productive and institutional units of society—not only factories, but the media too—will enable them to start solving these contradictions. It will produce new values, new identities; it will mold a new and essentially human culture as the people resolve old conflicts based on cultural and economic conditions. And at some point, there will be a qualitative change and the people will have transformed revolutionary intercommunalism into communism.

We call it "communism" because at that point in history people will not only control the productive and institutional units of society, but they will also have seized possession of their own subconscious attitudes toward these things; and, for the first time in history they will have a more rather than less conscious relationship to the material world— people, plants, books, machines, media, everything—in which they live. They will have power, that is, they will control the phenomena around them and make them act in some desired manner, and they will know their own real desires. The first step in this process is the seizure by the people of their own communities.

Let me say one more thing, though, to get back to your question. I would like to see the kind of communism I just described come into being, and I think it will come into being. But that concept is so far from my comprehension that I couldn't possibly name the contradictions that will exist there, although I am sure that the dialectics will go on. I'll be honest

45

with you. No matter how I read it, I don't understand it.

QUESTION: But I still don't see where the contradictions are going to come in.

NEWTON: I can't see them either because they are not in existence yet. Only the basis for them is in existence, and we can't talk about things in the blue, things we don't know anything about. Philosophers have done that too much already.

QUESTION: You are talking about this ideology of intercommunalism as part of the program of the Black Panther Party and telling us that the idea is to strive for unity of identity. Yet a few minutes ago you mentioned that the Party only accepts Blacks as members. That sounds like a contradiction to me.

NEWTON: Well, I guess it is. But to explain it I would have to go back to what I said earlier. We are the spearhead most of the time, and we try not to be too far ahead of the masses of the people, too far ahead of their thinking. We have to understand that most of the people are not ready for many of the things we talk about.

Now many of our relationships with other groups, such as the white radicals with whom we have formed coalitions have been criticized by the very people we are trying to help. For example, our offer of troops to the Vietnamese received negative reaction from the people. And I mean from truly oppressed people. Welfare recipients wrote letters saying, "I thought the Party was for us; why do you want to give those dirty Vietnamese our life blood?" I would agree with you and call it a contradiction.

But it is a contradiction we are trying to resolve. You see, we are trying to give some therapy, you might say, to our community and lift their consciousness. But first we have to be accepted. If the therapist is not accepted, then he can't deliver the message. We try to do whatever is possible to meet the patient on the grounds that he or she can best relate to, because, after all, they are the issue. So I would say that we are being pragmatic in order to do the job that has to be done, and then, when that job is done, the Black Panther Party will no longer be the **Black** Panther Party.

QUESTION: That brings up a related question in my mind. How do you view the struggles of women and gay people right now? I mean do you see them as an important part of the revolution?

NEWTON: We think it is very important to relate to and understand the causes of the oppression of women and gay people. We can see that there are contradictions between the sexes and between homosexuals and heterosexuals, but we believe that these contradictions should be resolved within the community. Too often so-called revolutionary vanguards have tried to resolve these contradictions by isolating women and gay people, and, of course, this only means that the revolutionary groups have cut themselves off from one of the most powerful and important forces among the people. We do not believe that the oppression of women or gays will end by the creation of separate communities for either group. We see that as an incorrect idea, just like the idea of a separate nation. If people want to do it, all right; but it won't solve their problems.

So we try to show people the way to resolve these problems: the vanguard has to include all the people. O.K.?

Identity

On the second day of the conference at Yale Erik H Erikson opened with a lengthy statement of his own position on the question of identity. This is abbreviated here.

ERIKSON: ... In my terms , I would say that the biggest problem facing a universal "people" today is the question of how wide an identity one can afford without becoming formless, ineffective, and lost, and how small must and can be genuine communalities, concrete living situations in which a wider identity finds its home in the here and now.

... So we will be interested in knowing what kind of world organization you foresee for your intercommunalism. What will be the smallest units and what the largest? And if I may end with a question which interests me right now to the point that I go around like Diogenes with a flashlight, what kind of adult, what kind of mature citizen, do you visualize as the intercommunalist? I know that we have been so preoccupied with the sons who want to kill their fathers that we have failed to take a really good look at the fathers who, always again, sacrifice their sons, who cast gods into the images of superfathers so that they will sanction the sacrifices of the sons. Maybe the adult partaking in a world-wide identity will need neither a father-image nor a god figure in that compensatory sense, but only an ideal of maturity as the symbolic guarantor of a universal adulthood. This, too, we must discuss in historical perspective.

NEWTON: Let me clarify something.

The Black Panther Party was formed in 1966, and at that time, as I mentioned yesterday, we thought of ourselves as nationalists. Now prior to 1966 I had been involved in many organizations and parties— the Black Muslims, for example, even though I did not join because I could never quite accept the mystical or religious aspect of it. But there were other organizations too. And even from the beginning I found it difficult to accept some of the Black nationalist ways: I tried to develop an attitude of great hatred for people, in this instance white people, and every time I thought I had that attitude all developed and internalized, my comrades would call me on the carpet about something. For example, sometimes I would do courteous things such as opening a door for a woman who happened to be white, and they would ask me why I had done that. When I did these things I would be criticized; but when I didn't do these things, I would feel a certain guilt about it. And I really felt that I should have hatred for all of these people generally because all of them had received some privileges from the fact that their foreparents had been robbers and rapists and so on.

I mention these personal things to give you some background. The Black Panther Party, from its very conception, was meant as an antiracist party. Even with our rhetoric, we made it very clear that we were against racism, that the purpose of our organization was to transform things so that racism would no longer exist and no longer affect us. I say this because Erik seems to think that the Party found it necessary to even hate some people at this stage in its development. There is something to that, of course, but I would like to point out one thing about hate. Love and hate are not opposites; they are on the same pole, and the opposite of both love and hate is indifference. It's difficult for a Black person in America to be indifferent, so you can imagine the kind of agony one goes through. It is difficult to be indifferent, but it is also difficult to love, you see. To be involved often means to hate, but because love and hate both grow from the same pole, there's love there too.

Now, of course, the Black Panther Party is not based upon hate. We feel that our revolutionary program must be guided by a feeling of love—armed love we sometimes call it. I don't like to use the word "love" again but the language is poor: maybe there should be a new word to express what I mean about involvement and acceptance.

QUESTION: I would like to raise something which has always been a source of deep personal conflict for me. I look at the United States and the ruling structure, and I do not like it. I do not like the violence and oppression I see here and in Vietnam and in practically every other country. Now I can see in an intellectual way that the only way to react against this violence is with more violence. But when I read the Panther paper and see words like "shoot to kill," well, I just can't relate to that either. So would you speak to the question of wanting to create a new world and a new universal humanity, and at the same time having to pick up a gun and shoot?

NEWTON: Well, as I said yesterday, the Black Panther Party is against violence and works for the day when it will no longer be necessary. We want to abolish all guns and all wars because we believe it better for people to resolve their differences without violence. But we are not idealists, and because we are not idealists we try to understand things in their material context. And until the actual conditions exist where defense with a gun is not necessary, we have to act appropriately. It is insane to ask the Vietnamese to lay down their guns when the American ruling circle is napalming them. It is insane to ask the underground operating in South Africa to put down their guns when Blacks there are treated like slaves. It is insane because you are asking people to suffer materially for an ideal that will not benefit them.

So we condemn violence, but we make a distinction between the violence of the aggressor and the self-defense of the people. During the years of slavery, for example, the slave master kidnapped people, split up their families, forced them to labor, shipped, tortured, and killed them, stole all the profit from their work. This was the actual material condition of their lives. So if the slaves revolted - and they did, many times - they were defending themselves against murder. This is what Frederick Douglass meant when he said {let me read this} :

"The slave is fully justified in helping himself to the gold and silver, and the best apparel of his master . . . Such taking is not stealing in any sense of the word. . . . Slave holders had made it almost

51

impossible for the slave to commit any crime known to the laws of God or to the laws of man. If he steals he takes his own; if he kills, he imitates only the heroes of the Revolution" [Douglass, 1995].

We translate that to mean that oppressors have no rights which the oppressed are bound to respect.

So we believe that people have to defend themselves: that is why we armed ourselves openly when we started the Party. We took this risk because we felt that the people had to be educated about the potential power of the armed Black community; and now that the example has been made, we are concentrating on helping the people develop things they will want to protect - the survival programs.

You see, Chairman Mao's quote that "political power grows out of the barrel of a gun" is misunderstood time and time again. Most people interpret this to mean that political power **is** a gun, but that's not the point. The verb in the sentence is "grows": political power **grows** from the barrel of a gun; it culminates in the people's ownership and control of the land and the institutions thereon. Mao's own practice shows this: he was not interested in spreading the Communists' influence through mobile guerrilla units, but he believed deeply in establishing political power.

So we believe that in order to get rid of the gun, it is necessary to pick it up. We believe that material conditions produce the violence of the aggressor and the self-defense of produce the violence of the aggressor and the self-defense of the victim, and that the people have a right and an obligation to resist attack upon their attempts to change the material conditions of their lives.

QUESTION: Maybe I feel that way in part because I have never had a gun picked up against me, but. . .

NEWTON: No, you haven't, because you are protected by the police and by the imperial army.

QUESTION: All right, part of my hang-up about picking up a gun is that I have never had it picked up against me. But what bothers me the most is this: I can see that the North Vietnamese people need their guns, but when I read the Panther paper I get the impression that it is indifferent to those people who have been killed. I mean the paper sometimes strikes me as a sort of scorecard.

NEWTON: Well, you know, the Vietnamese also shoot down airplanes. I have a ring at home made from an American airplane that was cut down over North Vietnam while attempting to bomb the Vietnamese with napalm and TNT. The Vietnamese use all the little scraps of the planes they cut down to make rings, and then they give these rings to their friends. Imprinted on the ring is the number of planes they have destroyed: I think the one I have has the number 1300 on it. We are very proud of the ring because we are proud that they are able to defend themselves with primitive weapons. They have even shot down helicopters with **rifles**.

But after the plane falls, the Vietnamese take the dead pilot and bury him, making sure to put flowers on his grave. According to one account I read, a reporter saw this happen and asked the people why they put flowers on the pilot's grave, considering that he was destroying their children and villages. And they answered that the pilot was a victim, an unconscious lackey of the ruling circle. The reporter said that when the Vietnamese down a plane, they weep for the victim and preserve his grave so that when the war is over his people can come and take him home.

We feel the same way. We have great compassion for people, and we really believe that the death of any person diminishes us because we are all involved in mankind. But we will not hesitate to use whatever force is necessary so that sanity might prevail and people keep their dignity.

You mentioned "universal identity" a little while ago. You know, it is interesting that when we were talking last night, the professor stated it was difficult for him, even though he is an immigrant like myself, to understand what I have been through. But I think that I, or most Black people, can understand the suffering the professor went through. Black people can understand it because they have always been rejected in this country. We have never felt that this country

54

was our home, and our internalization of Western values had made it impossible for us to feel at ease in Africa. Even knowing this, we are still nostalgic much of the time and feel that we would rather deal with the many cultural differences one finds in Africa than with the racism and exploitation here. But then we realize that the Africans are catching as much hell as any people in the world, and from the same controller too. Like the saying goes, "I went to the mountain to hide my face, but the mountain cried out, 'No hiding place!'" We cannot hide. So out of this experience of suffering and oppression, the Party tries to develop something of a universal identity.

You know, I stayed in solitary confinement for three years, and just before I got out they took me from the state penitentiary and put me back in the county jail on what they call "little death row." I had stayed on little death row for a month and a half before I was shipped to the isolation cell. There had been five people there then, all of them people the authorities expected to go to the gas chamber. And when I was returned there, prior to my release, two of the guys were still there, one of them Black and one of them white. They had gotten reversals too, but they had already gone through their second trials and had been sentenced to death again.

I felt alienated for the first time since being in prison, very alone and very sad. The first time, they were all going to death and I was going to jail, but now they were going to death and I was being released. I wanted to apologize to them for being released, even though I had to go through a second trial too, because why should I have been released while they were going to the death chamber? Why should the people have demanded my release and not theirs? Because of my identification with those men, I wasn't really released from prison – I will not be free until every one of them is out of the death cells, I'll still be there. And it is the same with the world. Unless we cultivate an identity with everyone, we will not have peace in the world.

ERIKSON: We certainly could stop with what you said right now, but I have to make it clear that when I referred to my status as an immigrant, I really meant to emphasize the opposite from what you inferred—especially when one considers how many immigrants have suffered profoundly. I did not suffer at all, except to the extent that one can get mighty anxious when one arrives here with a young family. I will never forget the moment when our ship first sighted that coldly competitive skyline of New York. The sight more or less puts you in a mental state of survivorship, both in the sense of having to accept, without looking back too much, the fact of your own survival abroad, and in the sense of being determined to survive as a family here, too. All this at first narrows your perceptiveness and, I'm afraid, your capacity to empathize with the struggling masses, until you have gained a foothold and a self-definition as American. And, as I said, I happened to be one of the select immigrants who comes with the right kind of professional equipment and, therefore, is given a special chance, and, in addition, is made to feel that he is bringing an alleviative technique needed for medical progress and progress in general. It was only when, in my clinical work, I found social interpretations inescapable, that I slowly became aware of the depth and cruelty of the social conflicts in this country.

QUESTION: I hate to bring up the idea, but it is totally possible and maybe even best that a revolution will happen in my lifetime so that my children will benefit from it. But it deeply concerns me at the same time, because whether I choose to be a part of it or not I am Black and my children will be involved—I will be the target of some retaliation. And the retaliation that may come will probably be similar to that which happened in Austria or Germany when the Gestapo routed out the Jews. It's all a matter of position. All Black people in the United States will be part of whatever happens. But how in your view do we raise our children or prepare them to be ready for this type of reaction? It's a bad question, but you see my confusion. We know that something is going to happen whether it is started by the Black Panther Party or someone else, and whatever happens we will be a part of it.

NEWTON: Yes, you will be part of it because everything is interconnected; and no matter how much they would like to, white people cannot run away from it either because they are definitely involved as a part of the species.

QUESTION: But in this country right now we are in the minority.

NEWTON: Yes, but there is only one world community. In the context of this country, we are a minority; but in the context of the empire, we are definitely a majority. We do not say this to give people hope but to show them the true nature of the world today.

We can set the best example for our children by showing them how to love and how to fight against things that jeopardize the freedom of the people. In spite of the racism in this country, in spite of the history of oppression against us, we have to show our children how to love and how to defend ourselves. The only way the people of the world can resolve the contradiction between love and defense is to reverse the dominance, at which point we can keep the love and get rid of the gun. This is why we talk in our paper about people exerting their power. We have been conditioned to believe that we should not defend ourselves, even though fifty million of us have been killed in this country; we have been taught that we should be very humble and act like little Jesuses.

Well, we do not accept that idealism. We accept things the way they are. The oppressed peoples of the world are only children now; they are children because they do not have power and do not control phenomena. For many thousands of years they were hardly recognized at all, except as the toiling masses; and it is only now, as Fidel says, that they are beginning to write their own history. As children, they would be wiped out like the Jews in the ghettoes of Nazi Germany; but as mature adults, they would take the way of the Jews in the Warsaw ghetto and keep their human dignity.

This is the conviction of the Party. We know that the people have to have control or else the people will always be children. The people must express their will to power, and we believe that their desire to do so is beyond good and evil.

QUESTION: Much of the impact of the Black Panther Party, and the focus of much of the criticism of the Party, has been your willingness to come out and say that you are prepared to defend yourselves. Some people say: Look, if you are truly revolutionary, then you shouldn't play your trump card by telling people what you are going to do, because then they are going to pick you off one by one.

NEWTON: You are now talking about strategy. Uncle Ho said that it is incorrect to publicize military strategy for military reasons, but that it is perfectly correct to publicize military strategy for political reasons. To judge the correctness of our actions, then, you must understand what we were trying to do.

We believe that only the people can expropriate power from the ruling circle here and bring about the necessary transition in the world. So our primary task has been to change the attitude of the people toward that power. Helplessness in the face of oppression is the first attitude that has to be changed, because the slave never expropriates power from the master until he realizes that the master is not God and is not bullet proof. And then it is necessary to teach the people that they do not have to accept life at the cost of the loss of their dignity, and the only way to do this is to offer them examples of people who say if they cannot be free, then they will die trying. We no longer go around with bandoliers and guns because we believe we have helped change that attitude. If we had never offered them an example like that, though, they would not know us now; we would never have become their true representatives and leaders. Now we are opening up a new front, speaking out and saying that we might do something to the slave master. We are put into jail for that. We are murdered in our sleep, as Fred Hampton was. We are framed, as Bobby and Ericka were. This goes on. But at the same time these acts have gained us the attention of the people, and the vanguard that does not have the attention of the people has no way of challenging their unconscious state.

MODERATOR: We have been at it three hours **now.** Let's break and see where we are tomorrow.

The first day of the Yale meetings had begun with Huey Newton's defining statement on intercommunalism; the second day had started with one from Erik Erikson on identity. On the third day all the participants around the table and the (swelling) groups of observers and supporters arranged in rough arcs around the long sides of the huge rectangular table in the library of Trumbull College were eager to get straight on with the question-and-answer session.

MODERATOR: All right, here we go. I sense a burning question over there.

QUESTION: Yes, I have a burning question for Mr Newton. I have been reading over some of the notes I have taken and, frankly, I really cannot find anything that's startling or new about revolutionary intercommunalism. It seems to me that the ideology is old. It substitutes new terms for old.

NEWTON: The **phenomenon** is new. It did not exist before.

QUESTION: But it really seems like a visionary ideology for such a materialist as you, and almost impractical.

NEWTON: You mean materialism is visionary?

QUESTION: No, no, that's not what I'm saying. I'm saying that this whole thing about a unified identity is visionary. You are saying that the whole world is linked and is reacting in a certain way to the American empire, and this seems to me a repeat of something that has been said before. So I am wondering why you think the notion is really new.

NEWTON: First of all, the Party does not steal ideas. It often synthesizes ideas and tries to put them to practice, which gives us a deeper understanding of the original idea. So maybe you should direct your question to Mr. Erikson, because he ...

ERIKSON: He steals ideas? [laughter]

NEWTON: No, no. But his subject is identity. He is talking about a universal identity; I am talking about a culture that is essentially human; and I am merely trying to show the relationship and the similarity between those two approaches.

QUESTION: I understand that Mr. Erikson should address himself to that point from a psychological perspective. But since the Party is supposed to have a program that will bring about this concept of intercommunalism, it should also take into consideration that ...

NEWTON: Excuse me, but you are missing the point. We are not bringing about the concept of intertercommunalism or even the fact of intercommunalism, Reactionary inter-communalism, which is the order of the day, was brought about by the ruling circles of American imperialism. I am just describing an actual system of relationships in the world today.

QUESTION: Then what approach does the Party take to intercommunalism. How do you relate to that fact?

NEWTON: We see ourselves as among the victims of reactionary intercommunalism. As victims, we resist; as materialists, we try to understand what our situation is in respect to it. We try to relate to it, therefore by educating the people to their real condition and engaging them in actions that will change that condition. We try to find out what reactionary intercommunalism is and then try to manipulate it in the people's favor.

QUESTION: How are you going to manipulate it? In what direction?

NEWTON: Well, the people of tlie world are manipulating it already by struggling against reactionary inter-communalism. There are battlefronts throughout Asia, Africa, Latin America, and there is turmoil in Europe now too. People are dissatisfied with the state of the world today and they are resisting.

And all of these struggles are against the American ruling circle in one way or another. Mozambique and Angola, for example, belong to Portugal, and liberation fronts are fighting in both places. But the Portuguese belong to NATO and Americans supply them with the weapons they use to enslave the Africans.

QUESTION: I think you may be a materialist, but it seems to me that you are not dealing with material conditions. You are dealing with a grand scheme which does not relate to me at all in a practical sense. I don't think anyone denies that there are disatisfied people in the world trying to do something about their lot, but what we are interested in is getting more specific feedback about what is going on here with the Panthers in this country.

NEWTON: You say you are concerned about the people in this country, but I would speculate that you are concerned about a particular group of people in this country. You keep saying, "Let's not talk about the Vietnamese", "let's not talk about the people in Angola and Mozambique", "let's not talk about Ericka and Bobby or any of the sufferings of the people": Let's talk about things that concern students at Yale? Is that it?

QUESTION: I don't want to avoid talking about Ericka and Bobby. I **want** to talk about Ericka and Bobby. That's the point.

NEWTON: Well, you can't talk about Ericka and Bobby without talking about the Vietnamese.

QUESTION: But we **have** talked about the Vietnamese.

64

We have talked about intercommunalism and the world and other countries and the future and just about everything else. But we have had practically no confrontation with things that are going on here now.

NEWTON: All right, then. There's no court today, so I invite you to come to the trial on Monday. I invite you there because I refuse to talk about Bobby and Ericka here. I'll talk about them in the courtroom and outside on the Green, where our talk might mean something. But I won't indulge in your desire to merely talk in a classroom about the possibility of Bobby and Ericka going to the chair. If I feel guilty about anything, it is speaking here when they are in the docks, you see. I always feel very uncomfortable outside of the bars—when I was released from death row, I left people there—and every time I have a happy day, every time I laugh, I feel somewhat guilty.

QUESTION: Well, in a sense you have said more about this whole thing in the last five seconds than you have in the whole two days before.

QUESTION: The question in a lot of our minds is not that there are in existence oppressed peoples. We can see that. What is bothering us has to do with Mr. Erikson's notion of pseudospecies. Take cultural groupings like youth or blacks or Vietnamese or Chinese or North Koreans: each of them is a pseudospecies in Mr. Erikson's terms. Now one bond they all have in common is the fact that they are oppressed; they have a kind of communality for that very reason. But what happens when you attain a level where that common bond no longer exists? Will people be happy? Will no one want to become the new ruling class? I guess we have a hard time imagining some future when people no longer want to control one another.

NEWTON: We believe that the primary motivating drive of people is a will to power, a drive to free themselves from both external and internal controls. But we do not believe that this drive necessarily ends in the domination of one group of people by by another: it is only because people lack knowledge and technology that their natural drive for control has been distorted into a desire for power over **people** rather than a desire for power over **things.**

So we **can** conceive of a time when people will not find it necessary to steal power from other people. Given a high level of technological knowledge, people will control the universe instead... and then they can resolve their differences peacefully.

QUESTION: In that connection, do you think we can gain control of our own environment? Do you think it is too late for any of this to ever come about?

NEWTON: Too late for what to come about?

66

QUESTION: Well, some people speak in very pessimistic terms about the whole environment of Earth. They say it will give out in a certain number of years because our resources have been so misused.

NEWTON: They may be correct. But when we talk about the capitalists' exploitation of nature— the kind of thing discussed in what is now called the Ecology movement—we often forget that people themselves are a part of the natural world. The mass murder of Blacks in Africa during the slave trade, all the depredations the Europeans committed in South America and the Caribbean, the genocide committed by Nazi Europe against the Jews, the Slavs, the gypsies, and, of course, against all people of color, are probably the greatest examples of the exploitation of nature by the capitalists. You know the greatest ecological crime being committed right now? The bombing of Vietnam. And we think that until the ecology movement starts recognizing these facts, it will remain largely irrelevant to the majority of people in the world.

People have always struggled against nature, and it is impossible for us who are struggling for the necessities of life, who have to set up our own survival programs, to talk about the struggle ending. The difference between us and the capitalists, though, is that we want a rational relationship with nature. We know that the capitalists have put us in a situation where nature cannot support us; and ... we cannot support nature either. So our struggle is twofold: we struggle to survive

67

and gain power over our environment, and we struggle to have a rational relationship with that environment. Like I've said, we are a part of nature ourselves, so we think the difficulties we have with the environment are all in the family, you might say, and can be solved without hostility. The capitalists are not part of that family. They are mad men and will destroy nature as well as us, so our struggle to survive and gain a rational relationship with the natural world is first directed toward getting rid of these mad men.

QUESTION: Do you think that the expropriator can be expropriated soon enough for all this to happen?

NEWTON: We will do everything in our power to see that it can.

ERIKSON: ... I have indicated, and I will repeat this here, that the identities of future men will always combine a sense of uniqueness inherited from a number of past liberations—whether religious, cultural or political and yet also a sense of universal communality which must always again find ways of guarding itself against monopolizers and usurpers.

Well, that was quite a mouthful. But, Huey, could you accept such a psychological statement as a counterpart to your political one?

NEWTON: Yes. We say that we would like to express our own individuality in a collective consciousness. One of our chief drives is to free the man as we bring him into the human community.

ERIKSON: Then I should add that my immigration to America is now part of me—and while I would not want to overlook the possibility that we may see things differently as a result, I also feel strongly that without that development called the United States of America and, yes, even the technological imperialism that we deplore so much when it oversteps the limits of human comprehension and compassion—that without it we would not sit here talking as we do. That means that we have a common faith (maybe only because one must have a faith in survival) that each pseudospecies and each empire in some dialectical way added new elements to a more universal sense of humanity.

NEWTON: Yes, and I would take that further and say that without imperialism there would be no reactionary inter-communalism, and without reactionary intercommunalism there would be no revolutionary intercommunalism; and so it follows that imperialism lays a foundation for world communism. It is necessary for imperialism to exist, even though we don't like it: that's the internal contradiction, you see. I would agree with that. I'm not happy about it, but that is the dialectics of the situation.

QUESTION: You know, most students seem to have this thing about following someone or something and not really becoming concerned themselves. And it seems to me that just your mere presence here, Mr. Newton, forces me to some kind of subjective analysis: there are certain things that I am going to have to do sooner or later, certain conclusions that I am going to have to reach for myself about this society and whether I want to fit into it or try to effect some type of change. It seems to me that everyone is sort of running away from themselves right now. I mean, it is easier to take what you were saying and to attack it than it is to look inward and try to reach something inside; and that's what seems to have been happening for the past two days. People are saying, "Well, Huey, what do you think about this?" and "Well, Huey, you are wrong about that"; and, you know, I can challenge you from ten different stances at once without ever having to face the basic question you are raising within myself. As far as I am concerned, though, this whole discussion is about alternatives—and I think your mere presence here is an alternative. I don't know.

QUESTION: I would like to comment on that too because it seems to me that Mr. Newton is very, committed to what he has been talking about and most of us just don't know how to be. He says that he's not an idealist, but at the same time he is willing to sacrifice his life for what he believes in. And let's face it, a lot of people do not want to commit themselves that far because they . . .

NEWTON: They'll commit themselves. Uncle Sam calls and they will be over on the soil of the Vietnamese people risking their lives and even giving up their lives. It's not a question of giving up your life. The real question is: For what cause will you give up your life?

We in the Black Panther Party will not give up our lives when the ruling circles call for us to do so. We would rather give up our lives trying to expropriate the ruling circles. Now I don't like having to make that choice, because I would rather see all of humanity resolving its contradictions by discussions like this. But it is idealistic to think we can do so now: the simple fact that people must fight to end division shows a low development at this time for all of mankind.

QUESTION: You have said several times that the Black Panther Party is mainly involved in an educational program. But I guess I don't really understand exactly what you **do** to relate to people on the human level, how you set yourselves up as examples of the kind of thing you are talking about. I mean, what do you actually **do**?

NEWTON: Well, we have what we call a ten-point program. It's called a survival program—survival until the people become more self-conscious and mature, because until then we are all in danger of genocide. Members of the Party spend most of their time setting up these programs and helping run them.

These programs are open to everyone in the community. We have health clinics; we have a busing program for parents and relatives and friends of prisoners who would not be able to visit the prison otherwise because they do not have the money; and we have clothing programs, especially on the East Coast because of the winter cold. Now these are reformist kinds of programs, but they have been integrated into the rest of our revolutionary program. We do them all over the country and we are expanding them. We know they won't solve the problem. But because we are interested in the people, we serve the people.

QUESTION: The question was raised several times yesterday and again today about whether the Panthers have been operating over the past few years more by political intuition or more by the ideology which has been described here. I suppose the answer to that has to be that you need both in order to get off the ground: you need political intuition, obviously, to get some sense of how to proceed, and, once started, you need an ideology to enable people to understand what you are doing.

NEWTON: Political science, not intuition. We have always had an ideology and have always attempted to practice our theory. We studied the situation from the very start; we had a program from the very start.

QUESTION: All right. But the ideology as you have spelled it out seems to me less relevant once you leave the stage where victims are actively resisting oppression and enter the stage of universal consciousness. Do you see what I mean? I am not sure that your ideology is nearly as useful in offering a blueprint for arriving at that future stage as it has been for getting out of the stage we are in. It seems to me this is what people mean when they keep asking you: Where do we go from here? The usefulness of your ideology is that it mobilizes an enormous amount of human energy against a rather rigid structure and a rather fixed set of situations. But we are not going to need that so much anymore, because . . .

NEWTON: The Vietnamese don't need it?

QUESTION: Now wait a minute. I'm talking about the future, the way the future is going to emerge. We have set up a system, a technological system which rests on science and which determines the kinds of interconnectedness that we will have to deal with. In the long run, we are going to have to manage an enormously complicated plant. And this creeates a different situation from the one in which we lived as men for five thousand years. We are all involved with a large, complex technical system which we have got to manage somehow or it will get control. And I guess what I miss in your ideology is some way of defining the new institutions, the new ideas, that will enable us to control that evolution. So my question is: How are we going to manage the plant? Have you been thinking about that?

NEWTON: Oh, yes. We are definitely thinking about it.

Revolution

At the end of March the same year, 1971, the two sociology lecturers who edited the transcripts of the New Haven tapes - J Herman Blake (from the University of California) and Kai T Erikson (from Yale) - met together again with Erikson and Newton in Newton's Oakland apartment.

Huey's apartment - twenty five stories above the homely reality of the streets where he grew up - commanded panoramic views: through the stark glass walls a vista of the bay; through cctv on the huge screen in the living room, an eye on the front door; and, through the telescope in the bedroom, the faint shapes of comrades moving around on the "little death row" in the county jail.

Four people sat around Huey's breakfast table, drinking coffee and whiskey into the small hours, a very different scene from the New Haven meetings. Yet in some ways these later meetings lacked the intimacy of the more overtly confrontational set-up at Yale where the great expanse of mahogany had provided a physical barrier over which the participants strained towards each other with a visible effort of will.

At the first of the Oakland meetings it was Kai who started the ball rolling.

KTE: We were talking about the meetings in New Haven ...

HPN: My preconception about the meeting was that I would be at odds with you, Erik, as a psychoanalyst. I didn't know that you had developed a new approach to the understanding of man's behavior. After I read a number of the essays and books you had written, I was impressed; your approach took the edge off of what I thought would be my attack, you see, because I was ready to view it as an adversary kind of thing. Then after starting the seminar at Yale, I was somewhat on the defensive because of the general environment. There were a number of people there who were more likely than not to misunderstand. And I was more likely than not to misunderstand, too, because in a setting like that you tend to want to answer as quickly as possible, to come out looking and feeling all right about it. In that kind of environment, one might miss the purpose of the whole thing.

EHE: I suggested to Kai that whatever title we agreed on [*for the book: Erikson and Newton, 1974*] the word "search" or "exploration" should be in it. We were really in an exploratory mood in New Haven, and that was the meaning of the whole thing. But, of course, I was on the defensive too—wondering from which direction your offensive was going to come, and feeling that we were an odd pair of contestants. We are obviously an old man and a young man, an immigrant to America and a Black man coming out of that American reality which I did not know and, no doubt, preferred not to know at first. And then, too, I am a psychoanalyst at the end of his career, a certified professor, already emeritus; and you are a young man who has put his life and liberty on the line in the service of a future as yet unclear to me. So on every score we were apt to talk **by** each other at first—which is actually what happened at the scheduled meetings, even though we were relating privately in ways I was not yet willing to share in public. When you come right down to it, I am the kind of person who has to **respond** to what is going on in the world with psychoanalytic insight, which I realize now you can accept up to a point. But I could not be **sure** when we first met that you would not feel like calling me some kind of names— because, you see, I thrived on that system that exploited your people, thrived in spite of being an immigrant, a former dropout, and (then no general recommendation) a Freudian. And then, just before we met, I had received a certain amount of publicity—my picture on the cover of magazines and all that—because a book about me had just come out. I felt particularly vulnerable then. My book on Gandhi is the closest I have come in understanding revolutionary action.

JHB: What was the role of the students in the conference? What were they looking for? What were they expecting?

KTE: I don't know. As I look back on the whole affair, I sometimes worry that I handled it poorly. It all began with a phone call from Don Freed, as I guess you know, and our thinking at the time was that it would be nice for you, Huey, and later for you, Pop, to compare ideas with one another in a room full of thoughtful students. I suppose I actually had two things in mind. For one, I am a teacher and I just wanted students to hear and share in the discussions. And then, frankly, I also wanted to avoid bringing a lot of other professionals into the conference who have their own particular lines of thought to offer—Yale is full of them, of course—because I thought our agenda would get so crowded. It seemed to me that "intercommunalism" and "the wider identity" were about as much as we could handle in a three-day workshop, and I did not want other people hawking their own wares. I didn't even hawk my own (to the great irritation of my esteemed colleague here) and maybe I was just too sensitive on that score. It might have been interesting to hear what people like Bob Lifton or Bill Coffin or Ken Keniston would have made of the proceedings.

EHE: In retrospect, would you have liked to have some of those people there?

HPN: I think it would have been interesting. I didn't think the students made the contribution they could have.

KTE: Well, one problem was that the conference got out of hand in terms of scale. If I had to do it over, I wouldn't locate the whole thing in that enormous library: it's Ivy League to the core. And there were simply too many people in the room. Several of the students I talked to felt they were in some kind of theater, acting out a script they hadn't seen yet.

JHB: Perhaps. But it seemed to me that the students were reflecting a general public attitude—an image of Huey

Newton and the Black Panther Party which is uninformed and unenlightened—and I really doubt that they saw the conference as an opportunity to become exposed to new ideas. I thought some of the students were surprised to see Huey without his shotgun. I would be interested in, knowing from you Erik, what your first reaction was to Huey's articulation of revolutionary intercommunalism. Is this the direction you expected him to come from? The reason I ask is that I have a concern which is shared by many persons who have become revolutionary. People who sit in positions of power and influence keep saying, "We're doing all right, what's the matter with you that you can't fit in?" They cannot seem to accept as legitimate the fact that someone has done an objective and serious analysis of the system they live in and has consciously made the decision not to be a part of it. For people like that, to even give serious thought to the ideas of the Party is to question their lives, their selves, their beings, their positions; and so they spend all their time trying to rationalize the matter, to push the Party back into the system or even to psychoanalyze it out of existence. I'm wondering to what extent those kinds of sentiments were coming through.

EHE: Well, as to that last point, I probably should have stressed earlier that the very fact of my being a psychoanalyst makes me hold back with criticism or critique. I've seen psychoanalytical explanations used as weapons - either of offense or of defense - only too often, and I have tried to learn not to do that. I want to first to understand the whole situation and then see where any psychoanalytic explanations might fit

79

in. So I guess I held back exactly in that area where, from your previous experience, you thought I might let go.

JHB Yes.

EHE: No wonder the students felt that neither of us really let go. They felt, I would imagine—and, Kai, you correct me if I am wrong—they felt that you, Huey, were so theoretical that they could barely recognize the man with the gun and wondered if you were holding back for reasons of academic environment. At the same time, they half-expected that I would light into you, asking about your background, your personality, in an effort to figure out the unconscious determinants of your revolutionary leanings —which, come to think of it, is what I did do in the case of Luther and Gandhi, but only after long study of their voluminous confessional utterances. So maybe the students felt a little betrayed: they came to a spectacle in which Huey was going to be aggressive and I was going to be psychoanalytic and the sparks would fly.

KTE: And that is certainly how we arranged the room: like a Roman spectacle.

EHE: They felt each of us betrayed our mandate, in a way, and that we overadjusted to those rows of books all around us.

KTE: I think that is partly so, but something else may have been going on at the same time. Most of the students I

80

know want to relate more closely to people they admire or are interested in. They wanted to hear a little more from each of you about who you are, what you are thinking, and how all of that is connected to the realities of their lives. But what they got was theory—and a pretty abstract brand of theory at that. They wanted to be responded to, accepted as deserving people, and I am not sure that they were.

EHE: I could make that clear to myself in terms of my own theory and say that first of all they wanted identify and then they wanted to understand. So they were mostly interested in challenging Huey—in finding out how they might identify with or against him and what he could mean to their identity choices.

KTE: That's it. They were more interested in coming to terms with Huey as a person than with intercommunalism as an idea, which certainly isn't hard to understand.

EHE: And that's their birthright, of course. We should remember, too, that one of their dominant conflicts right now is between being students in order to study for an occupation and a profession and a career, or being students so as to be informed activists in the meantime. I don't know what is going on at Yale right now, but when I came out here a month ago a number of professors at the University of California told me how depressed the students are because they don't see at this moment any genuine access to activism; and I'm not sure that we didn't get some of that conflict at Yale. You know what I mean?

HPN: Sort of ...

EHE: And when you, of all people, talked like a damned professor!

HPN: Well, they're not the only ones I have had **that** problem with.

JHB: But I wonder if that didn't paralyze them a bit.

KTE: It's funny. You know, a lot of people were upset because they thought we had chosen nothing but conservative students for the conference—and maybe they were in some abstract class sense—but in the Yale scheme of things a number of them were reckoned to be rather radical.

JHB: Well, we won't go into that.

KTE: How about radical with a small *r?*

JHB: No, I know what you mean. I think one of the things people don't understand or refuse to see is that the Black Panther Party is not just some willy-nilly, helter-skelter bunch of people who run around trying to upset everybody. It is a program, a distinct pattern of thinking and ideology, delivering certain conclusions from which strategies and actions derive. The ideology is critical here; revolutionary intercommunalism is a way of visualizing reality so that people can understand the critique the Panthers have been developing all along. It's not simply that Huey talks like a professor, which I wouldn't deny for a moment, but that people cannot accept the logic of what he says because they are not ready to go that far.

KTE: I suppose that's true too. But students have not really heard very much ideology before. Radical politics on campus has largely been a thing of action, movement, feeling, protest; students are just not accustomed to hearing anyone present a calm and reasoned ideological statement, no matter how revolutionary its thrust. That's one reason why the young white radicals these days and the older socialist radicals who learned their politics in the thirties and forties have such a hard time getting together. Have you heard very many serious ideological conversations on campus?

JHB: No, I haven't. I agree with you. A lot of students just do this and do that without thought, although it's understandable when you consider that they spend so much time in classrooms (I just though I'd toss that in) . But in my opinion, and in the opinion of some of the colleagues with whom I work very closely, revolutionary activity without serious planning and thought is in fact counterrevolutionary.

HPN: As a matter of fact, that's a very good statement about unplanned action—about revolutionary action and counterrevolutionary action. Young people generally feel that the role of the revolutionary is to define a set of actions and a set of principles that are easy to identify and are absolute. But what I was trying to explain to them was the **process:** revolution, basically, is a contradiction between the old and the new in the process of development. Anything can be revolutionary at a particular point in time, but most of the students don't understand that. And most other people don't understand it either.

JHB: What was your reaction, Erik, to Huey's original statement? I've always wondered about that.

EHE: I've wondered too. Much of it I simply didn't understand, to tell you the truth—or maybe I was just waiting for a combined personal and intellectual impression without which I do not "understand" Maybe what we just said should have been the very introduction to the whole thing, the relation of revolutionary action to revolutionary ideology and theory. ... there are a number of different passions in a revolutionary. Hot action is one of them, cold theory is another; and we been exploring the affinities of the two in political and psychological theory... Maybe I should have said then exactly what I said just now about the several passions that a revolutionary has; that all revolutionaries, even when armed, love to argue thing's in theoretical and ideological terms. Didn't you come to the meetings with the expectation that that was understood?

HPN: Not really. That's why I said in the beginning that we were dropouts and that the students would need more of an explanation because they wouldn't understand. Dropouts understand things students don't.

JHB: Erik, would you be a little more specific about what you expected?

EHE: Oh no, we have talked enough about that I just did not expect to hear a sermon on materialism as a theory. But why not? I was glad to listen. I should repeat, however, that I did expect others to participate more ...I definitely felt that there should have been a number of other approaches represented there to help fill in the spaces between the ideological and the psychological. I listened for where my concepts might fit in, and that's what I responded to on the second day. In the background, of course, there were always two great spirits, Marx and Freud. If we have any theoretical grandfathers in common, they are Marx and Freud— and maybe Darwin as well, but that's something else again. In historical perspective, the young Marx and the young Freud were much less far apart from each other than was the case when they became Marx and Freud. So if we could not resolve the relationship of materialism and psychology, we went on living that historical split. You must remember that where materialism entered psychology, it became behaviorism, which is not my field, and I think that one of the names I expected to be called was "idealist." So where does that leave us? Can one be a materialist psychologist without reducing everything to conditioned reflexes.

HPN: I would only consider a psychologist or a psychoanalyst an idealist if he attempted to explain the phenomenon of personality strictly in nonmaterial terms—in other words, if he did not acknowledge that the "spiritual" side of a person finds its genesis in a material source, you see. You would agree with that, wouldn't you?

EHE: Sure, I would agree with that...In the lives and struggles of revolutionaries, all kinds of unconscious motivations are obvious which, they must sooner or later recognize, have little to do with their professed rationales. In understanding such unconscious motivations, maybe one could avoid such destructive developments as where old comrades fight each other as mortal enemies. But maybe this is just a necessary part of the history of all revolutions—all **past** ones at any rate.

HPN: I remember we talked in New Haven about the necessity for contradictions, the reality of contradictions, in everything. It is the same with the social as it is with the physical and biological world. Old things clash and new things emerge, showing characteristics of both the old and the new.

EHE Now I wonder if I could turn to another topic entirely and ask you, Huey, to talk a little about the principle of inner contradiction. That is something that most people, including the students at Yale, do not get and are apparently not prepared to get. Where and how do we both use it? For example, I would say that a positive and a negative identity are a dialectical given in each person. But let's come to that later see what contradiction means in your sense and it could be clarified for people like the students. What has your kind of contradiction to do not only the dialectical but also with relativity and com-plimentarity? All this is hard for students. It's hard for everyone, really, but we have let the students stand for so many things in our conversations that they might as well represent "everyone" for the moment.

HPN: I don't think the students are taught dialectically, and one of the reasons they are not is that it would be detrimental to the bourgeois educational system to do so. I think it is a fair statement that the schools are agencies of the status quo: the bourgeoisie needs to train technicians and to give students a conglomerration of facts, but it would be detrimental for them to give students the tools to show that the status quo cannot stand and so to analyze them out of existence So I think it is more than just a question of students "having a hard time."

87

EHE: I even have a feeling that some of them did not understand what you meant by "idealism." They weren't sure whether you were talking about **ideas** or **ideals**. So when you spoke of contradictions, my feeing was that some thought it was something one must avoid, not something that is intrinsically necessary. It is very difficult for students to be asked to believe tliat we all are living contradictions—and cannot help it.

KTE: One difficulty here, it seems to me, is that Huey uses dialectics to deal with the emerging present, to discuss things that are in the process of becoming. Students and professors, on the other hand more often use dialectical reasoning to explain what happened in the past—why Hannibal acted as he did and so on. A lot of academics assume, without realy saying so, that one is free from a dialectical process she moment one understands it, you see what I mean? So **Huey** comes and tells everyone that they are a part of the very process they are talking about whether they want to be or not. That's pretty scary at twenty you know. It's scary at forty. Now you may be comfortable seeing your own views as transitory or the truth as you see it now as temporary, but most people are not. Not in the universities, anyway.

HPN: I don't know how comfortable I am, either.

EHE: We can't afford to forget how young these students are—which is why I reminded us all of the fantastic things you did, Huey, when you were in your early twenties. The students are looking—you know I even have a term for it, I call it "totalism"—they are looking for totalistic explanations and not for relativistic analysis. A total explanation is something you can totally identify with or against, a stable point of reference against which you can know where you are.

JHB: Yeah, but why do you think they are doing that, Erik?

EHE: I think they are doing it because that is part of being young—and I agree entirely with you that this is also what opens them up for a kind of complete indoctrination by some system. Some of them are quite willing to remain open, of course, but that is a scary state to be in.

HPN: The main thing I am saying is that they don't know how to go about it. And the reason they don't know how is because it is convenient for the schools not to teach them that. It's better to give them a conglomeration of facts to remember so that they can be used by whatever employer or profession they go into, and never step outside of it.

EHE: Maybe all of this has something to do with what you are trying to do in your course, Herman, when you speak of the complementarity (that's the word I would use, at any rate) of emotion and thought. You want the students to feel, right? But then you complain because you get so many papers in return that are emotional but not thoughtful. While what you really want to teach them is to feel and then to be able to stand back and think about what they felt.

JHB: Right.

EHE: And then to step back and see what kinds : feeling were in that thought. Isn't that what you in mind?

HB: That's the way I'm approaching that class, yes.

EHE: That is the way you are approaching that class but you must notice how hard it is for that age to do what you ask.

JHB: Yes. But I still think there is a more fundamental problem here. There are all these self-serving theories which seem to suggest that you reach a point where process stops, where transformation ends.

HPN: That's what happens when you get into power.

JHB: That's right, that's right. And what I am trying to say is that students see themselves as in process, in transition from childhood to adulthood; but they always want to know where the process stops. You see what I mean?

EHE: It is exactly at this point where my ideas about

identity are easily misunderstood as meaning that once you become identical with a role, then the process stops and you know where you are. That is why the most common way identity is represented is as an answer to the question "Who am I?"—a definition of identity I have never used and never would use. because the answer to the question "Who am I?" (if there really were one) would end the process of becoming itself. Real identity formation, of course, is continuous process with a special crisis in youth— and I would think, it is a dialectical process, which is what we may yet want to talk about.

KTE: Well. how about it, Huey? Does the dialectical process ever end?

HPN: I think that after the dialectical process has run its course, man will reach a state of godliness —and that's because I think God is mostly what man has said "I am not" Now that's just long-range speculation of course. We'll have to live with dialectics for a while yet.

EHE: Now about positive and negative identities? If you assume everybody has a set of self-images which he has learned he should strive for and a set of images he has learned he should avoid—and yet he is always both, because real identity cannot be anything but an interplay of these things. Now, would you call that dialectics?

HPN: Yes, I think that is a beautiful example.

91

EHE: You see, some students seem to hope that by studying my stuff they will learn what a positive identity is and how to get rid of the negative one. Another group of students is afraid of my stuff because they think what I mean by identity is to be so adjusted to the system that you don't want to be anything else but what the system permits you to be. And neither of these explanations represent what I meant. The trouble starts when you project your own negative identity on other people.

JHB: We have talked a lot about the meetings at Yale. I would like to change directions for a moment and go back to a matter that Erik has always been interested in: maybe it's time to talk about the gun.

EHE: Well, actually, that fits right in here. You see, when I started to talk in New Haven I reminded the students of the traditional image which Huey used to, represent and which still appears on the cover of the Panther paper—the young Black man with the gun. All of this became more dialectical in our conversations when you, Huey, began to speak about arms and love. I thought I understood what you meant to some extent because of something that became clear to Gandhi as he developed his nonviolent method—namely, that most people seem to feel that to be nonviolent means not to **have** any gun and not to **want** any gun because one would not want to use it or would not know how to use it anyway.

But there is an intermediary step between violence and nonviolence where you have a gun but use it only in the most disciplined way—in part, at least, to show up the absurdity of particular kinds of armed violence. This, I think, you did on several important occasions which really created your original public image. I hope you see now what I mean. You were not afraid to carry that gun. Now I would understand armed love to mean that one can really love only if one knows that one could and would defend one's dignity, for only two people of equal dignity can love each other. There is no use trying to love somebody who denies you dignity or to whom you deny it. In this sense, then, there is a dialectical relation between violence and nonviolence, and the last thing I would want to imply here is that your earlier image is inconsistent with the things you are saying and doing . Both together make up a historical step and (I would assume) a very personal step, and you needed the one for the other. I don't know whether you would agree to that. You would now accept the gun-carrying image wouldn't you, as historically necessary and valid.

HPN: I think it served a strategic purpose—although I imagine historians are going to make a lot out of it.

EHE: You mean like I just did?

HPN: No, no. It's just that so much has been written about the whole business of the armed self-defense of the community, and I haven't seen one thing that's accurate. I'm not talking about you, Erik; I think your interpretation is fair. But I just sort of shiver whenever I see books written on the matter.

EHE: For example, Bobby Seale describes some of the things you two did in the early days of the Party that, to me, seemed to amount to a parallel with the Gandhi technique — although I assume you didn't know about it then or, at any rate, it was not uppermost in your mind. When you faced down those policemen, for example — not threatening them with your guns or indicating with gestures that you would shoot first, but daring them to shoot first. That was a very important psychological condition you created there. You gave them the initiative and said, "O.K., you shoot first!"   All of this is probably related somehow to the old western frontier scenario, where the cowboys used to make this kind of confrontation a supreme test as to who would be quicker on the trigger. But you made something very different and, in a way, very revolutionary out of it when you made it clear that you didn't come to shoot them, but if they had come to shoot you, then they should come out with it. You paralyzed them morally, don't you think?

HPN: Well, I would agree that they were paralyzed at least.

KTE: But why were they paralyzed?

HPN: They had never been required to cope with a situation like that one. Because of their own racism, their own misconception of the black community and the black psyche, they did not know how to deal with the fact that we were not afraid of them, you see? And they were very provocative.

EHE: This kind of transvaluation can be a historical act, and Bobby Scale has a very good sense of how to describe such things— with humor, too. For example, how you would stand there with a few of ur men and would confront those policemen and all the armed power they had behind them. Now, of course, you shouldn't be surprised if they afterward should feel endangered in their essence. It has often been said about Gandhi that he could only have done what he did with the British and not anyone else. All of that fits rather well into what you refer to as the dialectical development of empires. You see, Gandhi met the British head-on with their own ideas of fairness, ideas they had widely established as an ideal, and when he faced them down with that they simply had to accept it as a lesson. It could well be that a policeman whose background does not include any kind of experience with this kind of thing would simply say to himself—"Okay, to hell with it, I'll get him some other time." What I learned in studying Gandhi was how he could give to a concrete object— and this is what I meant to apply to the gun in your case—some endless symbolic meaning. For example, when Gandhi announced that he was going to the Indian Ocean and take salt out of it, salt that the British were taxing, no matter what they say or do, it is perfectly obvious that he picked salt for many reasons. It is absolutely necessary in the tropics, for one thing, but it has great symbolic value too. Now my feeling is that, in principle, what you tried to do with the gun might have had something of the same concrete and symbolic meaning, and that you did it at the right historical moment. Does that make sense or not?

JHB: It makes perfect sense to me. I wish you would just be more specific, though. You used as a subtitle for the Gandhi book an expression like "the origins of militant nonviolence," and I think the concept of nonviolence as utilized by Americans with respect to Blacks is quite different from what I hear you saying?. It seems to me that nonviolence here has always meant acquiescence to whatever power is used against one in one's attempt- to gain justice. Some moral force would come from somewhere and overcome the violent application of force. I'm not sure that is what you are saying.

EHE: Not exactly. In fact, there is a similarity here which I brought out in the Gandhi book. It would be very easy to say that Black people have to remain nonviolent because they'll never learn to fight anyway, and some people would say, "Well, nonviolence fits their inborn meekness and their religious orientation" Now the case is very similar with India because there you have one military caste that had done virtually all the fighting, so that the great masses of people in India never learned to use weapons at all until the British came along and drafted them into the army. Those crack Indian

96

troops in the British Army that we heard so much about all came from warrior castes whose job on earth, decreed by heaven, was to fight. The rest of the Indians didn't know how to fight, had never had any experience with weapons, and made it a point of religious observance to do no harm to anyone. Now Gandhi (and his friends did not like him for it) would sometimes support the British demand that Indians be drafted, because he felt that Indians would have to learn to fight before they could **choose** to be nonviolent. That's what you meant in part, isn't it? That it makes no sense for a meek person to call himself nonviolent, because, sure, what else can he be?

HPN: I think it would be wrong to compare other situations to Gandhi's action. You have to leave it in context and regard it in terms of the particular contradictions involved. Now I would have agreed with the notion that Indians join the British Army in order to get the training necessary to oppose the army: I can understand that at some point it is worthwhile to play upon the weakness of the oppressor. Gandhi did this knowing the character of the British quite well, but I think he would have acted differently here. People here who tried to act the same way he did, I think, missed the mark and were not realistic.

JHB: Most people would say that the apostle of nonviolence in this country with respect to Blacks was Martin Luther King. He had a clearly stated philosophy and openly expressed a debt to Gandhi. Now I would suspect that most

97

people, not understanding the context in which you are speaking, would expect to see a very strong clash between your views and Huey's views on this particular subject. And I would like to see that cleared up, because I've always argued that there have to be certain social bases for nonviolence ...

EHE: Look, the last thing I would wish to do is advocate nonviolence outside of a concrete situation, particularly since it makes exploited people all the more vulnerable. Unless one is very careful, the whole nonviolent point of view could be used against people rather than for them. I gave a seminar at MIT once, and somebody brought Tom Mboya to one of the meetings. The students and I had just been discussing Gandhi, so we asked Mboya what he thought about nonviolence. Well, he said, you can use it with British but you can't use it with the Belgians. No historical situations are ever identical in this sense. What Mboya may have also meant was that Gandhi had become something of a Britisher himself: he had been educated in England, of course, and so he knew where he could count on the British to react to nonviolence in a certain way. I guess that is really all I have to say. I just have a feeling that you are not an advocate of violence as such, you know.

HPN: No, I don't advocate violence. I advocate nonviolence. If I really had a choice, I would prefer the nonantagonistic kind of contradictions because they usually can be resolved in a peaceful way. But of course we have to deal with concrete conditions and the reality of the situation at this time is that there are many contradictions that probably can only be resolved in antagonistic ways and will probably result in violence—and this will probably be the case until man and society develop to the point where contradictions will no longer be antagonistic. So I am working for the day when antagonisms will no longer exist. And this will probably be only after people commonly own and share things.

JHB: Erik, you were saying the other day that the Panthers may understand nonviolence better than anyone else because they understand violence so well. And I was thinking about that in connection with Huey's statement that we advocate the abolition of war. We say that power grows out of the barrel of a gun. Chairman Mao's words; but we also say that the purpose of picking up the gun is to get rid of it. Now most people in this society pick up the gun for the purpose of maintaining control, and they do not understand that someone else might pick it up in order to abolish control.

HPN: Use violence in order to eliminate it.

JHB: Right. Right.

EHE: The point is that you cannot step from un-disciplined violence to nonviolence. In India, Gandhi failed mostly where he could not restrain people from rioting, and you remember (I remember, at least) how he called off some of his nonviolent campaigns because rioting broke out. Now the Panthers have actually opposed violence for its own sake, isn't that right?

HPN: Nondisciplined violence, yes.

EHE: Only a very self-disciplined use of force can lead to disciplined nonviolence and the abolition of violence. And, of course, it also takes a pretty high set of moral aspirations for leaders to make people understand all of that. . . .

The four men continued their discussion for sometime before, Kai T Erikson, the radical white academic from Yale, author of the defining text on the sociology of exclusion [Erikson, K T 1968] realised that the tape had run out. He replaced the tape while the older white man went for a leak. Huey replenished the drinks.

KTE: O.K., the machine is on again. It's time for Oedipus and the controller.

HPN: Well, the Oedipus myth, as I understand it, is used in psychoanalysis as a symbol. The son competes for the mother's love and feels hostility toward the father because he keeps him from the mother. Now I concluded that it is not always the father *per se* but the **controller** in the house. The Oedipus complex is not so much a sexual drive as a drive to eliminate the controller or take control away from the controller. As a matter of fact, that is something we have to make quite clear: eliminating the controller and assuming the place of the controller are two different things, taking on the positive and casting off the negative.

EHE: Which would then be a dialectical kind of thing, right?

HPN: Right.

EHE: You love your father and you want to become like him, but at the same time you want to get rid of him so you can replace him. So it is built into a society that you end up being more or less like your father, and represent the same to your children. Now I gather you are saying that something happens in a revolution to change that repetitive pattern, but I can't quite see ...

HPN: That is exactly what I wanted to take note of. There's a difference between eliminating the controller and assuming control: it is possible to get rid of the controller without assuming all of his negative characteristics. One way is to not only eliminate the controller but all of his creations at the same time, although it shouldn't be done the way some people in the youth movement are doing it. It is a very immature thing to run away to communes and to plow the soil all over again—renouncing all of the technological equipment the father happened to produce because they oppose him. They are rejecting one manifestation of freedom if they do that, the freedom to choose whether to plow or not, you see.

EHE: O.K., would you also include in this a certain violent faction that seems to want to destroy the whole system so that it can be reborn? And these people are willing to sacrifice all technological achievements in order ...

HPN: To negate the whole thing. I didn't understand at the time, but Trotsky always talked about there being no such things as particular kinds of culture, there was only continuity. So at some times a gun is quite necessary and at other times it would be proper to use other strategies, whatever will promote the victims' move toward freedom. But the Oedipus complex is as much as anything else a symbolic fight of the victim against the controller.

EHE: I wrote a paper on dissent recently for the *International Journal of Psychoanalysis* and I took that occasion to point out that we always talk about the Oedipus complex as if only the boy's hostility was involved. But we never talk about Laius, the father of Oedipus, and ask what "complex" made him so ready to believe the oracle that his little boy was going to kill him someday. He believed it so strongly that he put the baby Oedipus out, exiled him. We won't understand the repetitiveness of this pattern unless we realize the importance of the fact that the king believed in the son's potential threat instead of trusting his own ability to bring up the little boy in such a way that the oracle would have been disproven. That would not make a myth, I know, but it might make history. Why do we not point to the ways in which every establishment and every established organization, out of a fear that the young will overcome them, limit the identities of the young and permit them access to adulthood only by way of confirmations, communions, inductions, and so on—every one of which limits the young to a particular identity and threatens transgressors? And, of course, war comes in here in the sense that every pseudospecies would put their young into particular uniforms and try to impress them by way of historical mythology that the highest affirmation of life would be a heroic death for the system. If you die well, you're going to be immortal— and all the more so if you first kill many representatives of the other pseudospecies *ad majoram gloria* of your own pseudospecies.

KTE: Who are also young

EHE: Who are also young. They kill each other off, then, and at the end the two systems make peace with each other, having killed enough of the best fighters in each other's younger generation to have avoided a certain potential for rebellion in their own country.

KTE: Boy. That's quite a thought.

HPN: Yes, it is.

EHE: There is something to that, don't you think? But nowadays the young of countries that a very short time ago were ready to do this to each other periodically, like the Germans and the French, are suddenly beginning to recognize that they are in many ways closer to each other than they are to their respective parents.

HPN: That is because they are becoming one community. That is what intercommunalism is all about.

KTE: The people to whom this is becoming most obvious—in this country, at least—are the young who realize that it is always other young people they go to war with, and Blacks who realize that is it usually exploited people they go to war with.

HPN: That's right.

EHE: ...You mentioned Trotsky: remember how - in spite of Lenin, who was probably the most balanced of all those men - in the end Stalin made of himself (again) the little father, the traditional "little father," heir to the Russian tradition with all its capacity for tyranny? ...The question always is: When you gain a new measure of freedom, who can claim the right to sanction it? The fact that man has such a long childhood may be the evolutionary origin of his tendency to always search for an older figure who will sanction whatever license he takes. Even if rebels first kill the father and then kill each other, there always comes the question—who is going to be that charismatic older brother who sanctions the license you took and confirms your right to have taken it? And then some of the brothers will fight each other for the role of the oldest. The result, as we can see even in some of the abortive revolutionary developments of today, can be paralysis, and then depression, lethargy and a re-emergence of the old moralisms in revolutionarv disguise; for man cannot destroy the old without some kind of sanction. I have a feeling that revolutions have been very costly for this reason—costly in a way that man today, with the means of mechanical destruction available to him, simply cannot afford. Let's just take Stalin as a historical example ... My God, what if he had had an atomic arsenal at his disposal? What might have happened then?

HPN: Well, what did happen? This country had the weapons, and look: Nagasaki, Hiroshima.

EHE: O.K. You've got me there. That's what we should talk about tomorrow—Hiroshima, the moon, and America. I would like to try out some notes on you.

HPN: You mentioned that revolutions are costly, and I just wanted to say that they are not themselves costly and negative: it's the kind of friction, the kind of obstacles that are in the way of revolution that keep the change at the antagonistic level, you see. But the process of revolution, the process of change, the new struggling against the old to produce some synthesis, does not necessarily have to be a destructive process.

EHE: Well, I hope you are right.

Universal Identity

On the following evening it was, again, Kai who clicked on the tape recorder and opened the discussion.

KTE: Could I start off by asking a question? One of the common grounds between Newton's ideology, Erikson's psychology, and the various notions that Herman and I bring in from the sociological outfield - he can play left field and I will play center - is the realization that a person's perception of reality is more or less shaped by the experiences he has had and by the position he occupies in the world. That's good dialectical materialism, good psychoanalysis, and good sociology all at once, right? Now we have made a lot of the fact that one of our principals is a seventy-year-old white man, an immigrant to this country, while the other is a thirty-year-old Black man who comes out of a very different set of circumstances. To be true to the logic of our various methods, then, we would have to say that these circumstances are the lens—if that is the word—through which we look at reality. I would like to hear each of you talk about those circumstances for a while.

HPN: I think it is easy for any person who accepts the ideology of dialectical materialism to share the methods and subject matters of all other disciplines, because all scientists are concerned one way or another with dialectics if they practice a true science. That's why I think that, despite age differences, the discipline of psychology and the approach of dialectical materialism would necessarily share many things in common—beginning with the developmental process and the recognition of the internal contradictions in all things. That is why it is not surprising to me, though it may be surprising to other people, that we could come to agreement on some things and at least discuss a number of things that are of interest to both of us.

KTE: Right. That's what my question is all about. There is a destination out there in the middle distance, let's say. Huey reasons his way to that destination by dialectics and Pop {Erik} reasons his way there by a more psychoanalytic kind of logic. We have talked a lot about how similar the destinations seem to be, but we have not said much about the different paths you took to *get* there—or about the different travelers, for that matter. See what I mean? Maybe the Harvard professor will say a word about the Yale professor's question.

EHE: Well, you are right. There are a number of things I didn't spell out when I talked about myself as an immigrant. During a lifetime like mine, one can actually witness the kinds of transformation which you, Huey, describe—contradictions meeting each other and change taking place. Now my experience is that even some of the most trite and commonplace characterizations of the American Dream hold psychologically and have to be taken care of in any American's self-appraisal. When one comes from Europe, America impresses one as the first self-made nation, creating itself out of immigrants who came from all the different pseudospecies of the world and converged here. They had to create a new nation and to become nationals of a new kind. And that nation became a new kind of industrial empire, certainly different from the British one. The British Empire created a superidentity too—we don't have to go into that—but at least there always was an England—an ancient geographical core, a self-contained island .

HPN: One empire is based upon tradition, the other empire is based upon technocracy—and that's a new kind of nation in itself.

EHE: But technocracy was not the original idea. The coming together of technocracy with a self-made nation was—in some ways, at least—almost a historical coincidence, even though a new nation with a whole wide continent to expand in had what it needed as the base of a new technocratic empire. Historically, then, the "self-made" idea and the technocratic vision fused into an idealized image of a man who almost literally made himself, created himself, manufactured himself, invented himself. This is important to point out because what we call the American empire is really a universal technocracy with America in the role not only of central power but also of central value-giver. And the main value we export is that of the self-made man. In Germany and Japan, for instance, people who belong to the establishment have to some extent accepted that basic value, and even in India you can see it reflected very sharply in the new managerial class. Compared to others, they look American, talk American, live like Americans in apartment houses, and are beginning to develop a new family structure and a new set of values to go along with it. Now I would argue that the self-made man is a new kind of pseudospecies—a type of person who by temperament and opportunity can make of himself pretty much what he wants to and who considers other pseudospecies to be people who cannot do all of that for reasons of race or class or type or weakness or something else. Of course, the Indians (American, this time) who happened to be situated here and the Blacks whose immigration was not exactly self-chosen were very useful to the image of a pseudospecies that likes to think they came here of their own free will—or by God's choice.

HPN: I would like to question the whole concept of the self-made man. The people who settled America were not self-made, but were the product of specific social and historical circumstances. The people who came to America were outcasts, they were victims; and the state they established was quite different from the traditional kind of empire. Now as we were saying a while ago, we can see that people sometimes— probably most of the time—arrive at a certain level of power without this power being shared in a universal sense. They become the new status quo and they attempt to hold back the process again. And once they try to stop the process of change they take on form of the father, of the controller. Only now, with a new kind of technocracy at their disposal—transportation, mass media, and so on—their influence is so great that they reach everyone in the whole world. Now this is dialectical in itself, because as their control becomes more severe and more encompassing, the more enemies they make. And this is why I say that the whole world has become one community in the hands of the old victim, who is now the new lord you see. This is reactionary intercommunalism. The downfall of this new self-made man, then, is going to be that people will rebel against him because of his insistence that he has all of the answers. This is why reactionary intercommunalism, while it causes its own destruction, also lays the foundation for its own transformation; because without modern communication and all the rest of it, how would the youth of the world develop a common identity? A sense of themselves as oppressed?

JHB: The point I have been trying to make is that the changes we are talking about require a new character definition, new definitions of self—but that is only going to come about as a result of hard, hard struggle. And those youth who are seeking a new identity must divest themselves of the old identity based on quantity and more quantity. I just don't see that as a very likely prospect.

EHE: I know. But to me, identity has to do with terrific power struggles as well as with terrific delusions. It is a matter of life and death, and not just a conscious choice of what kind of nice identity one would like to have. To me, identity means what the best in you lives by, the loss of which would make you less human. .. when you teach at Harvard today and you see the children of all those successful people, it is striking how little it means to them—or so they pretend—what their parents are. Now this is not just a fad, a passing mood: the fact is, I think, that they do not get from their parents' way of life the necessary identity strengths. Sosomething is happening across the nation—the world, for that matter—and maybe the Panthers have been in a key spot here in developing a strong and fraternal image.

KTE: I sense a pause. Could I steer you back to the question of how and where one's ideas originate?

EHE: Oh, that. Well, I gave a paper the other day for a meeting of scientists in Europe, each of whom were being asked why **they**, of all people, were the first to think of a particular word or concept or theory which afterward seemed so self-evident to everybody. And I was asked: Why were you the first to write about "identity crisis" in a systematic way? ... I came to this country at the time when it entered into something of an identity crisis, just because it had tried to make out of the descendants of so many different pseudospecies one new one. So the American identity was in some ways a manufactured one, a self-invented one, and . . .

112

HPN: And I would say that it is a necessarily oppressive one.

EHE: Well, all right, but so is every other identity that comes from the same source. Let me try to say it in one sentence, and then I will be through. As long as the core of any collective identity is a pseudospecies idea, it is going to be oppressive. As long as the Britishers felt chosen by God to colonize all those African and Asian countries, they were bound to be oppressive —although they did create a new conscience at the same time. America, too, for a long time could ignore the fact that it was bound to be oppressive in order to spread new ideas along with new methods of production.

HPN: But when we create a spirit of oneness, it won't be oppressive.

EHE: That is, I think, what Marx meant way back when he spoke of an overcoming of history itself, an idea probably related to that of the withering away of the state.

HPN: I think that you understand reactionary and revolutionary intercommunalism very well. You put it in somewhat different words, but I can agree with almost everything you say. Just before I went to Yale, I told the class at our Intercommunal Institute that I did not know how I was going to fare there because your writings had taken the wind out of my argument. I had thought at first that I would just be dealing with another psychoanalyst but after I read some of your things I found it difficult to treat you as an adversary. But at the same time, I felt that I could not just go there and agree with you because of my own situation in the Party. So you see the dilemma I was in. And I felt a little robbed, too, because I had worked very hard to put my ideas together, and here someone else had already laid a number of them out. That is somewhat frustrating, you know.

KTE: This may be the time for me to pursue my favorite question again, the one with which we began this morning. The way Huey hacked through the forest to arrive at the idea of communalism is very different from the way Pop hacked through the forest to arrive at the idea of identity, even if the two products look a lot alike. Now Pop said a word or two about the circumstances that could help explain why he was the person to write about identity and the identity crisis. So, Huey, why do you suppose you were the person to come up with the idea of intercommunalism? Would it be fair to ask you how you made your way through that forest?

HPN: Personally, I am not sure I know.

EHE: Why do you think you invented intercommunalism?

114

HPN: Well, I didn't invent it. I discovered it, focused upon it.

EHE: O.K. I didn't invent identity crisis either...

HPN: A scientist, if he is also an activist, will necessarily go about changing things in a different way than a laborer, let's say, or someone else who does not have any particular discipline, you see. So I went into activism with a scientific method, and .. .

EHE: But why? That's the point. There must have been something in your background, in your choice of parents, in the place where you grew up, which made you that independent. If you consider **only** how many of your brothers just accepted what they were taught, or accepted being excluded from what was being taught, while you always insisted on your right to study and your right to teach. There's always a personal quality to a man which cannot be reduced to explanations. That's obvious. But you must have some idea what . . .

HPN: Well, I don't know how important it is. I seldom discuss my own personal life except as it relates to the movement.

EHE: I seldom do either. In fact, I only talk about myself in relation to the identity concept... I think one has the right—maybe even the duty—to restrict oneself to that: otherwise everything becomes a kind of self-indulgence.

HPN: I think one of the things that would naturally make me somewhat freer to take an objective approach to situations rather than just follow what has been traditional is the fact that I am the seventh sibling in my family. I am the youngest and my family is very tightly knit; my father and mother have been married almost fifty years now, I guess. I was protected, you know, taken care of; and in a situation like that one is usually a little rebellious. In order to assert myself, I would act somewhat aggressive.

EHE: How many brothers and how many sisters?

HPN: Three brothers and three sisters. And, as I say, I was the youngest. It is almost a book in itself to tell you how I was torn between my brothers and my sisters. I took on the characteristics of all of them, in a way, and by doing that I was bound to be transformed, you see, because how could I identify with all of them and at the same time maintain the thing that was characteristic of the family? I could see, let's say, identifying with my father or my mother and coming out with the kind of personality that is either just the opposite or very much the same as either of them. But I developed a relationship with all of them and appreciated all of their personalities—and that made me different from them. It made me a stranger in a way.

EHE: But don't you think that as the youngest you were also very important to all of them and that they made you feel important? I would assume that this was so, in spite of the fact that the youngest always feels oppressed because the others are so big.

HPN: Well, I felt loved by everyone in the family. Not necessarily important, but loved.

EHE: Was it clear from the outset—obviously it became clear later—that you were going to be the last child also? How old was your mother when you were born?

HPN: Well, she was fourteen when she was married. She must have been around twenty-nine when I was born. Maybe thirty or thirty-two.

EHE: And how about that move west to Oakland? Oakland seems important to me somehow, but I can't figure out why.

HPN: You know, I didn't leave Oakland until after I got out of prison except for two trips to Los Angeles. I didn't leave for the whole twenty-five years. I came here when I was one or two years old.

EHE: Do you think Oakland has something to do with all of this? Oakland and the West?

HPN: As a social scientist, I would say that wherever we are has a definite influence on us, and what we have to do is find out the difference between one area and another.

EHE: Well, you probably know what I am driving at. I have been impressed, as I said more than once, that there seems to be a strong Western influence in the Black Panther image.

JHB: I was just thinking about the time the idea of intercommunalism came into the picture. I remember coming over to your place, Huey, the day that you started talking about intercommunalism, and I can say very honestly that I have rarely seen you as excited as you were then. You told us that it was a vision. But if you look at it in terms of its materialistic basis, it was a vision which came as the result of trying to put together a lot of different concepts in some comprehensive way. You were handling and juggling a lot of them then.

HPN: That's right. I was not satisfied with a statement that I was writing to the Vietnamese because there was a contradiction in it. Let me share this with you. I was telling the Vietnamese that the Party supported their nationalism, their revolutionary nationalism, even though we were not nationalists. We were internationalists and could not be nationalists: no Americans could afford to be nationalists because we are all guilty on one level or another of being the exploiter or accepting the bribe of the exploiter if we are not at war with him. So I said that I disclaim nationalism because it is a thing of the past but that I would support their nationalism nonetheless. I disclaimed all of the black nationalists in that statement —and, of course, that brought about a bad relationship between our Party and other black organizations because all of them, even the bourgeois ones, are somewhat nationalistic in tone and in goal. Now if we disclaim nationalism for ourselves and vet support nationalism for those other people, then it seems as though we are belittling them, being traitors to them. So I sent the statement to them, but I was very dissatisfied and unhappy for about a month. I kept tossing this around in my mind and suppressing it in a way. Then I woke up one morning witli this concept of intercommunalism, and it was like a vision: it didn't seem as coldly calculated as when you work out a mathematical problem, which is how I usually handle things intellectually. I just woke up that morning and I had solved the contradiction in my sleep. And I was excited to get it out. I have had the experience in the past of having a dream or vision and then forgetting the damn thing because I didn't get it down. I was anxious to get all of this down in writing so that I could refer to it. And that is the history of that concept.

EHE: Now you are a revolutionary and I obviously am not...

HPN: Some people say I'm not either.

EHE: But, as you say, several of our ideas are complementary in the sense that even though one can only go so far in bringing them together, they still relate closely to one another. Let me illustrate what I mean by relating what you have been saying to some concerns of mine about children and education. It is terribly important for communalism that children should live in a true community in order to develop a sense of identity that is communally based as it were. Identity is both an individual and a communal concept because you cannot have a sense of identity—or better, you cannot grow a sense of identity step for step through the life stages—without anchoring it somewhere in a group setting. Children, obviously, have only a fragmentary capacity to understand the world. At first, the child's mother is the world, and then he learns to interact with a limited number of people at given times.

HPN: At first, only with himself.

EHE: But even there, way back at the beginning, everything depends upon the way he is handled, the way he is nursed, all of which already expressed a community's style—so in that sense, he is never alone. Even the way the mother gives him the breast already expresses a communal style, because in different communities people do such things differently—what they **say** when they do it, how **long** they do it, the **way** they do it, and so on. There the child has already begun to be a member of the community. So much depends upon the parents' relationship to the rest of the community, too. For example whether the community gives them a peaceful and purposeful sense of administering to small children. I would say, then, that in intercommunalism groups would have to be interrelated sufficiently to assure children a sense of identity in a wider world, which could only happen if the rest of the world developed a common style of bringing up the children.

HPN: Yes, this is what would be necessary to stop the antagonistic kind of contradiction on the group or tribal or national level. But the only point I want to emphasize now—and I know you understand it—is that the process is usually very bloody because the identity that is forced on people is often based on hostility. . . . When I was young and working in the Black Muslims and other organizations, we were required to hate all white people. I would find myself being courteous to whites, and they would call me to check on it. Now I could understand intellectually and academically that I had the right to treat whites as roughly as I wanted, because they had the upper hand; but I would just find myself reacting differently. One time I saw a girl at one of our functions who was extremely light skinned with Caucasian features, and she kept trying to convince them that she was Black. They wouldn't hear her. They abused her and said she was really disturbed, you know, and she kept telling them that she was from Louisiana and wasn't white. It really hurt me. The tone was one of hostility the moment she walked in the door. Maybe I can relate that back to my family, I don't know; but within my family the cue was never color because there is a big difference of color in it. I remember that when I was a baby—I was just on the sideline then—my brother and sister would call one of my sisters "Red" when they got angry with her, and she would break down in tears. At the same time, some of the others would call the darkest one in the family a black bitch, you see, and then she would be broken up. My father had very straight hair and others had very curly hair, like my own. So I never thought that color was the way to tell people apart. I knew the difference between white people and black people, of course, but the cue was always the way white people treated us, not the color itself. Do you see what I mean? Maybe that was one of my problems in the early stages of the movement. Even now I would say that intercommunalism has something to do with this.

JHB: What you are saying is that you did not sense hostility from some whites and therefore you did not respond to them with hostility.

HPN: No, I'm saying that even if I expected and received a hostile kind of response from whites in most situations, my feeling would be related to something other

122

than the fact that they happened to be very light skinned, you see. So when a girl came in who looked white to me, I was willing to accept her as a Black the minute she said she wasn't white. I didn't care how light skinned she was. Herman, do you remember the hang-ups people like Malcolm X and Garvey had about skin color? Well, I can appreciate their concern about it, but this never affected me, you see what I mean? Because of the nature of oppression and the way the world is today, people identify each other by color. The {Black} Muslims personify the whole thing by saying that "white is evil," you see, and this is the kind of thing that is hard for me to accept. . . What I'm saying is that I need something else than color to judge people. For example, I often open doors for people without even noticing that they are white or giving it a thought; but I can be very, very hostile toward someone if he gives any indication whatever of feeling superior. Now most white people had a kind of opposition to me just because I am Black, you see, so they have their cue but I do not have mine.

EHE: May I ask one question? You spoke of your particular place in the family. Did your family have a particular place in the community?

HPN: Yes, we were victims. My father is an educated man, no formal education, although he is a very wise man. We were from a farming community and before I was born my father was a sharecropper. He married very early: my mother was fourteen and he was eighteen. Then he moved here to Oakland with seven children right after I was born and worked in the shipyards. My father always had at least three jobs to support the family, and that's another part of my own rebellion: I don't have a family and I probably never will.

EHE: Was your father somewhat different from the rest of the community? Did you perceive him as typical or unique?

HPN: Well, one of the problems my father had with people was that he was very light skinned with straight hair, and they could say that he was different from other Blacks. He would take exception to that, though, and say that he was no different and would rather be treated like every other member of his group. He would not accept any favors. He told us later that foremen on jobs would say, "You don't want to do this work, the other guys can do it; you can be truck driver." But he would say, "No. I'd rather not be a truck driver; I'll sweep the streets." So people attempted to treat him differently, but he would not accept it.

EHE: Well, then, he was different in not letting them **make** him different.

HPN: Of course.

EHE: So in many ways you came from a more stable family than most Blacks do.

HPN: My father went up to about eighth grade or so. He's not professional, although he has many skills. He lays brick, he's a cement mason, and he's a carpenter; but he does not have any credentials, so he would have to do all of this for a handyman's price. As I said, he would work three jobs to take care of seven children. He was a stable figure and we always depended upon him. My mother has never worked— she was always in the house having children or taking care of them—so he would have to do everything; pay all the bills, do three jobs, everything. Now I may be searching again for explanations, but one of the reasons I do not have a family or ever hope to have one other than the Party is that I have always identified with the sufferings of my father. I felt that he was captured. All he would do is work, and then he would send me around Oakland to pay all of the bills until the money was gone. This would happen every two weeks, and I decided that I would never be a slave like that. He was a slave, you see. He did it because he loved us, and we in turn loved him; but at the same time I rebelled against it. ...

KTE: So the Party will be your family?

HPN: The Party requires a good deal of sacrifice, but in order to sacrifice you need love. You know, Herbert Hendin has pointed out in a recent book that Black suicide is different from white suicide: 80 percent of all Black suicides occur, he says, because of the lack or loss of a lover—although I would

125

just want to say lack or loss of love in general. Whites commit suicide because they suffer the loss of prestige or position or economic security, but Blacks commit suicide for lack of love because this is all we have. If love is gone, there is no reason to go on—and this is how I feel about the Party. I am willing to make any sacrifice, not because of a suicidal tendency on my part, as some psychologists and sociologists have concluded, but because the sacrifice is compensated through the fraternity. But then the question arises at this stage of the game: what happens after the fraternity is broken, you see? Where's the reinforcement going to come from?

EHE: Well, that brings us back to the whole question of the fraternal and fratricidal relations of revolutionaries.

HPN: Is that a necessary part of development though?

EHE: The matter of brothers and sisters forming a community is a theme in all development, I suppose, but it seems to become an acute problem of leadership in revolutions. I watched you on television the other day when your old friend [Eldridge Cleaver] broke with you, and I couldn't help thinking (you may not want to discuss this here at all): what do brothers do to each other once it becomes a matter of struggling for power among equals?

HPN: The struggle for power among the brothers may be a natural outgrowth of eliminating the father, but it will

126

probably hurt more than the struggle between the son and the father because divorce is sharper. It is more devastating. But I don't know if I agree with you that this is a natural kind of outgrowth. I just don't know.

EHE: I didn't mean that. What I mean is that different historical situations bring out different aspects of man's learned patterns. And if this is so, then maybe it would be better to understand those patterns in order to control them better. There can be such a waste of human resources when the simplest emotions are misunderstood.

HPN: I think it would be fair to state that there is no real difference between familyhood and tribalism and no real difference between tribalism and nationhood. They all depend upon a sense of identity that is exclusive, you see—and this is even true of what they call internationalism.

JHB: When you say there is no difference, do you mean there is no difference in principle or in kind between, say, tribalism and nationhood?

HPN: There is only a quantitative difference between familyhood and tribalism and between tribalism and nationhood, not a qualitative difference.

JHB: But relationships between people in a family setting and a tribal setting are much more primary, whereas in a national setting they are more likely to be secondary.

HPN: I agree. It's impossible to have a face-to-face relationship between one hundred or two hundred million people. But it's still a matter of degree. At first, people say: "I will defend my family and serve my family because we share a common history, a common value system, a common ethnic background, and a common religion." Then as society grows a number of families come together in a close relationship, and say: "We have the same past, the same values— we are a tribe" Then the tribes compete with one another for territory until they merge into nations and it's the same thing all over again on a different scale: I will defend my nation because we share a common background, common principles and values," and so on. I would say that the concept of the nation is strictly related to the concept of the family, and that there is only a quantitative difference between the two.

JHB: So what is the next step?

HPN: Well, in order for man to survive there has to be some universal identity that extends beyond family tribe, or nation—an identity that is essentially human and does not depend upon people thinking that others are something less than they are.

EHE: The trouble with that comparison is that the family is essentially meant for bringing up children, while nations . . .

HPN: You are saying that the family is the traditional method for bringing up children. I would say that the family has always been a traditional way of keeping people children.

KTE: Huey, when we were talking about the Oedipus complex a little while back, you said something about science and religion that intrigued me.

HPN: Science constantly challenges the whole idea of the supernatural and God is, you know, the symbol of the father. Now once you reach a maturity in consciousness, then you assume the role of God yourself. Whenever science discovers something new, all of a sudden the church starts to say that it is now an earthly thing: it is not related to God anymore, but God still exists. So when does God stop existing? He stops existing as soon as you bite the fruit of knowledge and can assume control yourself. But you haven't really destroyed God; you have become God. You have become the controller yourself. The point is that a **will to power** is tle primary drive of man, not the sexual drive. It is an attempt to reverse the dominance in nature—to become the controller, to become the father, to become God. As long as other people control us. we remain children. As Erik pointed out, that is why Marx said that there can be no real adults in a capitalist society.

EHE: On the subject of controllers and fathers: what is happening right now to the leaders of the revolution in a wider sense? What form do you expect leadership to take in the future?

HPN: I think in the future people will realize more and more that they are responsible for creating leadership just as they are responsible for creating God. Groups create leaders just as they create other things, but they usually lose their awareness that this is so and begin to feel that the leaders are external to them, somebody to whom they must submit. So I would think that in the immediate future leadership will take more the form of the "chairmanship" — and in the distant future, although I can't really visualize it yet, leadership will become a coordinated effort among people and maybe even titles or statuses will no longer be necessary.

EHE: You know, we seem to be talking around things again. I don't quite understand your concept of God, for one thing. Obviously, to say that somebody or something is the father of all people is to say that all people are brothers: the common father guarantees the brotherhood. So one question we should keep in mind is whether brotherhood can survive the loss of fatherhood. In your Party, you use terms like "brother" and "sister," but you really don't have much in the way of father images, do you? The leaders of the Party look and sound more like older brothers in your publications. Of course Ho Chi Minh comes in every once in a while . . .

HPN: But they call him **Uncle** Ho.

EHE: See? They call him Uncle, the father's brother. Now how about Mao, is he a father image? He seems so much more like a grandfather—who, in fact, is trying to weaken any new consolidation of father images in the hierarchy. Is that right?

HPN: Yes.

KTE: The next question has to be: Huey, how does a leader like you manage to avoid becoming a "father" when you get older? How do you avoid that kind of imagery in a movement that sooner or later is going to embrace two or maybe even three generations?

HPN: Who knows? Everything is in a state of transformation, nothing is stable, and the Party, too, will be transformed.

KTE: But the kind of imagery the Party uses is going to have to change to take your old age into account.

EHE: There is something very simple to be said here which is that both a father and a god are irreversible. You cannot say that somebody is an ex-father—either he was a father or he wasn't—and nobody can be an ex-god. But then there are other forms of leadership, aren't there, and being a teacher is one of them. I am impressed how much Mao played the role later on of the teacher, the leader who would formulate things like the sages of old.

JHB: Well, Huey, I would say that you are more of a teacher than a leader or a father figure—a teacher in the sense that your approach is to provide people with processes by which they can arrive at answers rather than give them the answers themselves. That is what you are doing when you talk about states of change, internal contradictions, processes of development, transformations, and so on.

EHE: Can I ask one last question? Huey, what do you think of the two-party system?

HPN: Well, if there were a two-party system, maybe I would think well of it.

EHE: O.K. I was just thinking about constitutional rights, existing constitutional rights. Would you expect intercommunalism to change the political structures of the various countries?

HPN: Yes, I would. I believe that contradictions will be around for quite some time yet. I won't say "forever," because that's an absolute, but I cannot stretch my imagination far enough to see a time when contradictions will no longer exist.

What I do look forward to is the time when contradictions will be nonantagonistic, and I don't think that will occur until we resolve the question of property—of the property class and the class that owns no property, of the haves and the have-nots, of the contradictions based on economic interests. I feel that to resolve those contradictions it will be necessary to have a redistribution of wealth. Revolutionary intercommunalism will exist when power is distributed on an intercommunal level and each community of the world has control of its own institutions.

Self-Determination

The following translation is taken from Volume 20 of the English Edition of V.I. Lenin's <u>Collected Works</u> (Progress Publishers, Moscow, 1947). Written between February and May, 1914, Lenin's analysis, like Newton's, takes the form of a dialogue across a particularlistic divide, not this time skin colour with its ideological connotations, but an equally biological irrelevance - gender.

Whereas Huey faced Erik in person, Illych took on Rosa Luxemburg from the virtual safety of his writing desk. It is as well to note that, despite the patronising, pedantic tone of his criticisms, Lenin held "our Rosa" in great esteem and respect – perhaps even affection.

Clause 9 of the Russian Marxists' Programme, which deals with the right of nations to self-determination, has given rise lately to a crusade on the part of the opportunists[1]. There is no doubt that this campaign of a motley array of opportunists against our Marxist Programme is closely connected with present-day nationalist vacillations in general. Hence we consider a detailed examination of this question timely. We would mention, in passing, that none of the opportunists has offered a single argument of his own; they all merely repeat what Rosa Luxemburg said in her lengthy Polish article of 1908-09, "The National Question and Autonomy".

What Is Meant by the Self-Determination of Nations?

Naturally, this is the first question that arises when any attempt is made at a Marxist examination of what is known as self-determination. What should be understood by that term? Should the answer be sought in legal definitions deduced from all sorts of "general concepts" of law? Or is it rather to be sought in a historico-economic study of the national movements?

It is not surprising that the {afore-mentioned opportunists} did not even think of raising this question, and shrugged it off by scoffing at the "obscurity" of the Marxist Programme, apparently unaware, in their simplicity, that the self-determination of nations is dealt with, not only in the Russian Programme of 1903, but in the resolution of the London International Congress of 1896. Far more surprising is the fact that Rosa Luxemburg, who declaims a great deal about the supposedly abstract and metaphysical nature of the clause in question, should herself succumb to the sin of abstraction and metaphysics. It is Rosa Luxemburg herself who is continually lapsing into generalities about self-determination (to the extent even of philosophising amusingly on the question of how the will of the nation is to be ascertained), without anywhere clearly and precisely asking herself whether the gist of the matter lies in legal definitions or in the experience of the national movements throughout the world.

135

A precise formulation of this question, which no Marxist can avoid, would at once destroy nine-tenths of Rosa Luxemburg's arguments. This is not the first time that national movements have arisen in Russia, nor are they peculiar to that country alone. Throughout the world, the period of the final victory of capitalism over feudalism has been linked up with national movements. For the complete victory of commodity production, the bourgeoisie must capture the home market, and there must be politically united territories whose population speak a single language, with all obstacles to the development of that language and to its consolidation in literature eliminated. Therein is the economic foundation of national movements. Language is the most important means of human intercourse. Unity and unimpeded development of language are the most important conditions for genuinely free and extensive commerce on a scale commensurate with modern capitalism, for a free and broad grouping of the population in all its various classes and, lastly, for the establishment of a close connection between the market and each and every proprietor, big or little, and between seller and buyer.

Therefore, the tendency of every national movement is towards the formation of **national states**, under which these requirements of modern capitalism are best satisfied. The most profound economic factors drive towards this goal, and, therefore, for the whole of Western Europe, nay, for the entire civilised world, the national state is **typical** and normal for the capitalist period.

Consequently, if we want to grasp the meaning of self-determination of nations, not by juggling with legal definitions, or "inventing" abstract definitions, but by examining the historico-economic conditions of the national movements, we must inevitably reach the conclusion that the self-determination of nations means the political separation of these nations from alien national bodies, and the formation of an independent national state.

Later on we shall see still other reasons why it would be wrong to interpret the right to self-determination as meaning anything but the right to existence as a separate state. At present, we must deal with Rosa Luxemburg's efforts to "dismiss" the inescapable conclusion that profound economic factors underlie the urge towards a national state.

Rosa Luxemburg is quite familiar with Kautsky's pamphlet *Nationality and Internationality*. (Supplement to *Die Neue Zeit* No. 1, 1907-08; Russian translation in the journal *Nauchnaya Mysl*, Riga, 1908.) She is aware that, after carefully analysing the question of the national state in §4 of that pamphlet, Kautsky arrived at the conclusion that Otto Bauer "**underestimates** the strength of the urge towards a national state" (p. 23 of the pamphlet). Rosa Luxemburg herself quotes the following words of Kautsky's[2]:

"The national state is the form **most suited** to present-day conditions, (i.e., capitalist, civilised, economically progressive, as distinguished from medieval, precapitalist, etc.); it is the form in which the state can best fulfil its tasks" (i.e., the tasks of securing the freest, widest and speediest development of capitalism)".

To this we must add Kautsky's still more precise concluding remark that states of mixed national composition (known as multinational states, as distinct from national states) are "always those whose internal constitution has for some reason or other remained abnormal or underdeveloped" (backward).

Needless to say, Kautsky speaks of abnormality exclusively in the sense of lack of conformity with what is best adapted to the requirements of a developing capitalism.

The question now is: How did Rosa Luxemburg treat these historico-economic conclusions of Kautsky's? Are they right or wrong? Is Kautsky right in his historico-economic theory, or is Bauer[3], whose theory is basically psychological? What is the connection between Bauer's undoubted "national opportunism", his defence of cultural-national autonomy, his nationalistic infatuation ("an occasional emphasis on the national aspect", as Kautsky put it), his "enormous exaggeration of the national aspect and complete neglect of the international aspect" (Kautsky)— and his underestimation of the strength of the urge to create a national state?

138

Rosa Luxemburg has not even raised this question. She has not noticed the connection. She has not considered the **sum total** of Bauer's theoretical views. She has not even drawn a line between the historico-economic and the psychological theories of the national question. She confines herself to the following remarks in criticism of Kautsky:

"This national state is only an abstraction, which can easily be developed and defended theoretically, but which does not correspond to reality. [*Przeglad Socjaldemokratycny*, 1908, No. 6, p. 499.]

And in corroboration of this emphatic statement there follow arguments to the effect that the "right to self-determination" of small nations is made illusory by the development of the great capitalist powers and by imperialism. "Can one seriously speak," Rosa Luxemburg exclaims, "about the 'self-determination' of the formally independent Montenegrins, Bulgarians, Rumanians, Serbs, Greeks, partly even the Swiss, whose independence is itself a result of the political struggle and the diplomatic game of the concert of Europe?!" The state that best suits these conditions is "not a national state, as Kautsky believes, but a predatory one". Some dozens of figures are quoted relating to the size of British, French and other colonial possessions.

After reading such arguments, one cannot help marvelling at the author's ability to misunderstand the how and the why of things. To teach Kautsky, with a serious mien, that small states are economically dependent on big ones, that a struggle is raging among the bourgeois states for the predatory suppression of other nations, and that imperialism and colonies exist—all this is a ridiculous and puerile attempt to be clever, for none of this has the slightest bearing on the subject. Not only small states, but even Russia, for example, is entirely dependent, economically, on the power of the imperialist finance capital of the "rich" bourgeois countries. Not only the miniature Balkan states, but even nineteenth-century America was, economically, a colony of Europe, as Marx pointed out in *Capital*, Kautsky, like any Marxist, is, of course, well aware of this, but that has nothing whatever to do with the question of national movements and the national state.

For the question of the political self-determination of nations and their independence as states in bourgeois society, Rosa Luxemburg has substituted the question of their economic independence. This is just as intelligent as if someone, in discussing the programmatic demand for the supremacy of parliament, i.e., the assembly of people's representatives, in a bourgeois state, were to expound the perfectly correct conviction that big capital dominates in a bourgeois country, whatever the regime in it.

There is no doubt that the greater part of Asia, the most densely populated continent, consists either of colonies of the "Great Powers", or of states that are extremely dependent and oppressed as nations. But does this commonly-known circumstance in any way shake the undoubted fact that in Asia itself the conditions for the most complete development of commodity production and the freest, widest and speediest growth of capitalism have been created only in Japan, i.e., only in an independent national state? The latter is a bourgeois state, and for that reason has itself begun to oppress other nations and to enslave colonies. We cannot say whether Asia will have had time to develop into a system of independent national states, like Europe, before the collapse of capitalism, but it remains an undisputed fact that capitalism, having awakened Asia, has called forth national movements everywhere in that continent, too; that the tendency of these movements is towards the creation of national states in Asia; that it is such states that ensure the best conditions for the development of capitalism. The example of Asia speaks **in favour of** Kautsky and **against** Rosa Luxemburg.

The example of the Balkan states likewise contradicts her, for anyone can now see that the best conditions for the development of capitalism in the Balkans are created precisely in proportion to the creation of independent national states in that peninsula.

Therefore, Rosa Luxemburg notwithstanding, the example of the whole of progressive and civilised mankind, the example of the Balkans and that of Asia prove that Kautsky's proposition is absolutely correct: the national state is the rule and the "norm" of capitalism; the multinational state represents backwardness, or is an exception. From the standpoint of national relations, the best conditions for the development of capitalism are undoubtedly provided by the national state. This does not mean, of course, that such a state, which is based on bourgeois relations, can eliminate the exploitation and oppression of nations. It only means that Marxists cannot lose sight of the powerful **economic** factors that give rise to the urge to create national states. It means that "self-determination of nations" in the Marxists' Programme cannot, from a historico-economic point of view, have any other meaning than political self-determination, state independence, and the formation of a national state.

The conditions under which the bourgeois-democratic demand for a "national state" should be supported from a Marxist, i.e., class-proletarian, point of view will be dealt with in detail below. For the present, we shall confine ourselves to the definition of the concept of "self-determination", and only note that Rosa Luxemburg **knows** what this concept means ("national state"), whereas her opportunist partisans **do not even know** that.

The Historically Concrete Presentation of the Question

The categorical requirement of Marxist theory in investigating any social question is that it be examined within **definite** historical limits, and, if it refers to a particular country (e.g., the national programme for a given country), that account be taken of the specific features distinguishing that country from others in the same historical epoch.

What does this categorical requirement of Marxism imply in its application to the question under discussion?

First of all, it implies that a clear distinction must be drawn between the two periods of capitalism, which differ radically from each other as far as the national movement is concerned. On the one hand, there is the period of the collapse of feudalism and absolutism, the period of the formation of the bourgeois-democratic society and state, when the national movements for the first time become mass movements and in one way or another draw **all** classes of the population into politics through the press, participation in representative institutions, etc. On the other hand, there is the period of fully formed capitalist states with a long-established constitutional regime and a highly developed antagonism between the proletariat and the bourgeoisie—a period that may be called the eve of capitalism's downfall.

The typical features of the first period are: the awakening of national movements and the drawing of the peasants, the most numerous and the most sluggish section of the population, into these movements, in connection with the struggle for political liberty in general, and for the rights of the nation in particular. Typical features of the second period are: the absence of mass bourgeois-democratic movements and the fact that developed capitalism, in bringing closer together nations that have already been fully drawn into commercial intercourse, and causing them to intermingle to an increasing degree, brings the antagonism between internationally united capital and the international working-class movement into the forefront.

Of course, the two periods are not walled off from each other; they are connected by numerous transitional links, the various countries differing from each other in the rapidity of their national development, in the national makeup and distribution of their population, and so on. There can be no question of the Marxists of any country drawing up their national programme without taking into account all these general historical and concrete state conditions.

It is here that we come up against the weakest point in Rosa Luxemburg's arguments. With extraordinary zeal, she embellishes her article with a collection of hard words directed against § 9 of our Programme, which she declares to be "sweeping", "a platitude", "a metaphysical phrase", and so on without end. It would be natural to expect an author who so admirably condemns metaphysics (in the Marxist sense, i.e., anti-dialectics) and empty abstractions to set us an example of how to make a concrete historical analysis of the question. The question at issue is the national programme of the Marxists of a definite country—Russia, in a definite period—the beginning of the twentieth century. But does Rosa Luxemburg raise the question as to what historical period Russia is passing through, or what are the concrete features of the national question and the national movements of that **particular** country in that **particular** period?

No, she does not! She says absolutely nothing about it! In her work you will not find even the shadow of an analysis of how the national question stands in **Russia** in the present historical period, or of the specific features of Russia in this particular respect!

We are told that the national question in the Balkans is presented differently from that in Ireland; that Marx appraised the Polish and Czech national movements in the concrete conditions of 1848 in such and such a way (a page of excerpts from Marx); that Engels appraised the struggle of the forest cantons, of Switzerland against Austria and the Battle of Morgarten which took place in 1315 in such and such a way (a page of quotations from Engels with the appropriate comments from Kautsky); that Lassalle[4] regarded the peasant war in Germany of the sixteenth century as reactionary, etc.

145

It cannot be said that these remarks and quotations have any novelty about them, but at all events it is interesting for the reader to be occasionally reminded just how Marx, Engels and Lassalle approached the analysis of concrete historical problems in individual countries. And a perusal of these instructive quotations from Marx and Engels reveals most strikingly the ridiculous position Rosa Luxemburg has placed herself in. She preaches eloquently and angrily the need for a concrete historical analysis of the national question in different countries at different times, but she does not make the least attempt to determine what historical stage in the development of capitalism Russia is passing through at the beginning of the twentieth century, or what the **specific features** of the national question in this country are. Rosa Luxemburg gives examples of how **others** have treated the question in a Marxist fashion, as if deliberately stressing how often the road to hell is paved with good intentions and how often good counsel covers up unwillingness or inability to follow such advice in practice.

Here is one of her edifying comparisons. In protesting against the demand for the independence of Poland, Rosa Luxemburg refers to a pamphlet she wrote in 1898, proving the rapid "industrial development of Poland", with the latter's manufactured goods being marketed in Russia. Needless to say, no conclusion whatever can be drawn from this on the question of the right to self-determination; it only proves the disappearance of the old Poland of the landed gentry, etc. But

Rosa Luxemburg always passes on imperceptibly to the conclusion that among the factors that unite Russia and Poland, the purely economic factors of modern capitalist relations now predominate.

Then our Rosa proceeds to the question of autonomy, and though her article is entitled "The National Question and Autonomy" in general, she begins to argue that the Kingdom of Poland has an **exclusive** right to autonomy (see *Prosveshcheniye,* 1913, No. la). To support Poland's right to autonomy, Rosa Luxemburg evidently judges the state system of Russia by her economic, political and sociological characteristics and everyday life—a totality of features which, taken together, produce the concept of "Asiatic despotism". (*Przeglad* No. 12, p. 137.)

It is generally known that this kind of state system possesses great stability whenever completely patriarchal and pre-capitalist features predominate in the economic system and where commodity production and class differentiation are scarcely developed. However, if in a country whose state system is distinctly pre-capitalist in character there exists a nationally demarcated region where capitalism is **rapidly** developing, then the more rapidly that capitalism develops, the greater will be the antagonism between it and the precapitalist state system, and the more likely will be the separation of the progressive region from the whole — with which it is connected, not by "modern capitalistic", but by "Asiatically despotic" ties.

Thus, Rosa Luxemburg does not get her arguments to hang together even on the question of the social structure of the government in Russia with regard to bourgeois Poland; as for the concrete, historical, specific features of the national movements in Russia—she does not even raise that question.

There are many pages in this vein, where Lenin discusses the concrete historical specifics in Great Russia, Poland and the Scandinavian countries. He enjoins us to fight our own (national) bourgeoisie and landlords, to,

"fight their 'culture' in the name of internationalism, and, in so fighting, 'adapt' to the special conditions... that is your task, not preaching or tolerating the slogan of national culture".

On Jewish Nationalism

In the process of outlining this prescription Lenin addresses the specifics of both Jewish and Irish nationalism. On the Jewish question he states:

The same applies to the most oppressed and persecuted nation—the Jews. Jewish national culture is the

148

slogan of the rabbis and the bourgeoisie, the slogan of our enemies. But there are other elements in Jewish culture and in Jewish history as a whole. Of the ten and a half million Jews in the world, somewhat over a half live in Galicia and Russia, backward and semi-barbarous countries, where the Jews are **forcibly** kept in the status of a caste. The other half lives in the civilised world, and there the Jews do not live as a segregated caste. There the great world-progressive features of Jewish culture stand clearly revealed: its internationalism, its identification with the advanced movements of the epoch (the percentage of Jews in the democratic and proletarian move-ments is everywhere higher than the percentage of Jews among the population).

Whoever, directly or indirectly, puts forward the slogan of Jewish "national culture" is (whatever his good intentions may be) an enemy of the proletariat, a supporter of all that is outmoded and connected with **caste** among the Jewish people; he is an accomplice of the rabbis and the bourgeoisie. On the other hand, those Jewish Marxists who mingle with the Russian, Lithuanian, Ukrainian and other workers in international Marxist organisations, and make their contribution (both in Russian and in Yiddish) towards creating the international culture of the working-class movement— those Jews, despite the separatism of the Bund[5], uphold the best traditions of Jewry by fighting the slogan of "national culture". Bourgeois nationalism and proletarian internation-alism — these are the two irreconcilably hostile slogans that correspond to the two great class camps throughout the capitalist world, and express the two policies (nay, the two world outlooks) in the national question.

On Irish Nationalism

Lenin makes the same point in respect of the Irish question.

. . . let us return to the question of Ireland.

Marx's position on this question is most clearly expressed in the following extracts from his letters:

"I have done my best to bring about this demonstration of the English workers in favour of Fenianism. ... I used to think the separation of Ireland from England impossible. I now think it inevitable, although after the separation there may come federation." (This is what Marx wrote to Engels on November 2, 1867.)

In his letter of November 30 of the same year he added:

"... what shall we advise the *English* workers? In my opinion they must make the *Repeal of the Union* [Ireland with England, i.e., the separation of Ireland from England] (in short, the affair of 1783, only democratised and adapted to the conditions of the time) an article of their *pronun-ziamento*. This is the only legal and therefore only possible form of Irish emancipation which can be admitted in the programme of an **English** party. Experience must show later whether a mere personal union can continue to subsist between the two countries....

"... What the Irish need is:

"1) Self-government and independence from England;

"2) An agrarian revolution. . . ."

150

Marx attached great importance to the Irish question and delivered hour-and-a-half lectures on this subject at the German Workers' Union (letter of December 17, 1867).

In a letter dated November 20, 1868, Engels spoke of "the hatred towards the Irish found among the English workers", and almost a year later (October 24, 1869), returning to this subject, he wrote:

> "*Il n'y a qu'un pas* [it is only one step] from Ireland to Russia. . . . Irish history shows what a misfortune it is for one nation to have subjugated another. All the abominations of the English have their origin in the Irish Pale. I have still to plough my way through the Cromwellian period, but this much seems certain to me, that things would have taken another turn in England, too, but for the necessity of military rule in Ireland and the creation of a new aristocracy there."

Let us note, in passing, Marx's letter to Engels of August 18, 1869:

> "The Polish workers in Posen have brought a strike to a victorious end with the help of their colleagues in Berlin. This struggle against Monsieur Le Capital—even in the lower form of the strike—is a more serious way of getting rid of national prejudices than peace declamations from the lips of bourgeois gentlemen."

The policy on the Irish question pursued by Marx in the International may be seen from the following:

On November 18, 1869, Marx wrote to Engels that he

had spoken for an hour and a quarter at the Council of the International on the question of the attitude of the British Ministry to the Irish Amnesty, and had proposed the following resolution:

"Resolved, that in his reply to the Irish demands for the release of the imprisoned Irish patriots Mr. Gladstone deliberately insults the Irish nation;

"that he clogs political amnesty with conditions alike degrading to the victims of misgovernment and the people they belong to;

"that having, in the teeth of his responsible position, publicly and enthusiastically cheered on the American slaveholders' rebellion, he now steps in to preach to the Irish people the doctrine of passive obedience;

"that his whole proceedings with reference to the Irish Amnesty question are the true and genuine offspring of that *policy of conquest*[9], by the fiery denunciation of which Mr. Gladstone ousted his Tory rivals from office;

"that the General Council of the International Working-men's Association express their admiration of the spirited, firm and high-souled manner in which the Irish people carry on their Amnesty movement;

"that this resolution be communicated to all branches of, and workingmen's bodies connected with, the International Workingmen's Association in Europe and America."

On December 10, 1869, Marx wrote that his paper on the Irish question to be read at the Council of the International would be couched as follows:

> "Quite apart from all phrases about 'international' and 'humane' justice for Ireland—which are taken for granted in the International Council—*it is in the direct and absolute interest of the English working class to get rid of their present connexion with Ireland.* And this is my fullest conviction, and for reasons which in part I can *not* tell the English workers themselves. For a long time I believed that it would be possible to overthrow the Irish regime by English working-class ascendancy. I always expressed this point of view in the *New York Tribune* (an American paper to which Marx contributed for a long time]. Deeper study has now convinced me of the opposite. The English working class will *never accomplish anything* until it has got rid of Ireland.... The English reaction in England had its roots in the subjugation of Ireland." (Marx's italics.)

Marx's policy on the Irish question should now be quite clear to our readers. Marx, the "Utopian", was so "unpractical" that he stood for the separation of Ireland, which half a century later has not yet been achieved.

What gave rise to Marx's policy, and was it not mistaken?

At first Marx thought that Ireland would not be liberated by the national movement of the oppressed nation, but by the working-class movement of the oppressor nation. Marx did not make an Absolute of the national movement,

153

knowing, as he did, that only the victory of the working class can bring about the complete liberation of all nationalities. It is impossible to estimate beforehand all the possible relations between the bourgeois liberation movements of the oppressed nations and the proletarian emancipation movement of the oppressor nation (the very problem which today makes the national question in Russia so difficult).

However, it so happened that the English working class fell under the influence of the Liberals for a fairly long time, became an appendage to the Liberals, and by adopting a liberal-labour policy left itself leaderless. The bourgeois liberation movement in Ireland grew stronger and assumed revolutionary forms. Marx reconsidered his view and corrected it. "What a misfortune it is for a nation to have subjugated another." The English working class will never be free until Ireland is freed from the English yoke. Reaction in England is strengthened and fostered by the enslavement of Ireland (just as reaction in Russia is fostered by her enslavement of a number of nations!).

And, in proposing in the International a resolution of sympathy with "the Irish nation", the Irish people, Marx advocated the **separation** of Ireland from England, "although after the separation there may come federation".

What were the theoretical grounds for Marx's conclusion? In England the bourgeois revolution had been consummated long ago. But it had not yet been consummated in Ireland; it is being consummated only now, after the lapse of half a century, by the reforms of the English Liberals. If capitalism had been overthrown in England as quickly as Marx had at first expected, there would have been no room for a bourgeois-democratic and general national movement in Ireland. But since it had arisen, Marx advised the English workers to support it, give it a revolutionary impetus and see it through in the interests of **their own** liberty.

The economic ties between Ireland and England in the 1860s were, of course, even closer than Russia's present ties with Poland, the Ukraine, etc. The "unpracticality" and "impracticability" of the separation of Ireland (if only owing to geographical conditions and England's immense colonial power) were quite obvious. Though, in principle, an enemy of federalism, Marx in this instance granted the possibility of federation, as well, if only the emancipation of Ireland was achieved in a revolutionary, not reformist way, through a movement of the mass of the people of Ireland supported by the working class of England. There can be no doubt that only such a solution of the historical problem would have been in the best interests of the proletariat and most conducive to rapid social progress.

Things turned out differently. Both the Irish people and the English proletariat proved weak. Only now, through the sordid deals between the English Liberals and the Irish bourgeoisie, is the Irish problem being "solved"(the example of Ulster shows with what difficulty) through the land reform (with compensation) and Home Rule (not yet introduced). Well then? Does it follow that Marx and Engels were "Utopians", that they put forward "impracticable" national demands, or that they allowed themselves to be influenced by the Irish petty-bourgeois nationalists (for there is no doubt about the petty-bourgeois nature of the Fenian movement), etc.?

No. In the Irish question, too, Marx and Engels pursued a consistently proletarian policy, which really educated the masses in a spirit of democracy and socialism. Only such a policy could have saved both Ireland and England half a century of delay in introducing the necessary reforms, and prevented these reforms from being mutilated by the Liberals to please the reactionaries.

The policy of Marx and Engels on the Irish question serves as a splendid example of the attitude the proletariat of the oppressor nations should adopt towards national movements, an example which has lost none of its immense **practical** importance. It serves as a warning against that "servile haste" with which the philistines of all countries, colours and languages hurry to label as "Utopian" the idea of altering the frontiers of states that were established by the violence and privileges of the landlords and bourgeoisie of one nation.

Unity against Imperialism

Lenin reminds us over and over again to attend to the historical specifics, to support all struggles against capital in our own nations and in those of oppressor nations, concluding that,

The conclusion . . . is clear: the working class should be the last to make a fetish of the national question, since the development of capitalism does not necessarily awaken **all** nations to independent life. But to brush aside the mass national movements once they have started, and to refuse to support what is progressive in them means, in effect, pandering to **nationalistic** prejudices, that is, recognising "one's own nation" as a model nation (or, we would add, one possessing the exclusive privilege of forming a state).

Again and again Lenin returns to the basic resolution as passed by the London International Congress in 1896

This resolution reads:

"This Congress declares that it stands for the full right of all nations to self-determination (**Selbstbestimmungsrecht**) and expresses its sympathy for the workers of every country now suffering under the yoke of military, national or other absolutism. This Congress calls upon the workers of all these countries to join the ranks of the class-conscious (**Klassenbewusste**—those who understand their class interests) workers of the whole world in order jointly to fight for the defeat of international capitalism and for the achievement of the aims of international Social-Democracy."

Internationalism

Imperialism is the highest stage in the development of capitalism. In the foremost countries capital has outgrown the bounds of national states, has replaced competition by monopoly and has created all the objective conditions for the achievement of socialism. In Western Europe and in the United States, therefore, the revolutionary struggle of the proletariat for the overthrow of capitalist governments, and the expropriation of the bourgeoisie is on the order of the day. Imperialism forces the masses into this struggle by sharpening class contradictions on a tremendous scale, by worsening the conditions of the masses both economically—trusts, high cost of living—and politically—the growth of militarism, more frequent wars, more powerful reaction, the intensification and expansion of national oppression and colonial plunder. Victorious socialism must necessarily establish a full democracy and, consequently, not only introduce full equality of nations but also realise the right of the oppressed nations to self-determination, i.e., the right to free political separation. Socialist parties which did not show by all their activity, both now, during the revolution, and after its victory, that they would liberate the enslaved nations and build up relations with them on the basis of a free union—and free union is a false phrase without the right to secede—these parties would be betraying socialism.

Democracy, of course, is also a form of state which must disappear when the state disappears, but that will only take place in the transition from conclusively victorious and consolidated socialism to full communism.

The Socialist Revolution and the Struggle for Democracy

The socialist revolution is not a single act, it is not one battle on one front, but a whole epoch of acute class conflicts, a long series of battles on all fronts, i.e., on all questions of economics and politics, battles that can only end in the expropriation of the bourgeoisie. It would be a radical mistake to think that the struggle for democracy was capable of diverting the proletariat from the socialist revolution or of hiding, overshadowing it, etc. On the contrary, in the same way as there can be no victorious socialism that does not practise full democracy, so the proletariat cannot prepare for its victory over the bourgeoisie without an all-round, consistent and revolutionary struggle for democracy.

It would be no less a mistake to remove one of the points of the democratic programme, for example, the point on the self-determination of nations, on the grounds of it being "impracticable" or "illusory" under imperialism. The contention that the right of nations to self-determination is impracticable within the bounds of capitalism can be understood either in the absolute, economic sense, or in the conditional, political sense.

159

In the first case it is radically incorrect from the standpoint of theory. First, in that sense, such things as, for example, labour money, or the abolition of crises, etc., are impracticable under capitalism. It is absolutely untrue that the self-determination of nations is **equally** impracticable. Secondly, even the one example of the secession of Norway from Sweden in 1905 is sufficient to refute "impracticability" in that sense. Thirdly, it would be absurd to deny that some slight change in the political and strategic relations of, say, Germany and Britain, might today or tomorrow make the formation of a new Polish, Indian and other similar state fully "practicable". Fourthly, finance capital, in its drive to expand, can "freely" buy or bribe the freest democratic or republican government and the elective officials of any, even an "independent", country. The domination of finance capital and of capital in general is not to be abolished by **any** reforms in the sphere of political democracy; and self-determination belongs wholly and exclusively to this sphere. This domination of finance capital, however, does not in the least nullify the significance of political democracy as a freer, wider and clearer **form** of class oppression and class struggle. Therefore all arguments about the "impracticability", in the economic sense, of one of the demands of political democracy under capitalism are reduced to a theoretically incorrect definition of the general and basic relationships of capitalism and of political democracy as a whole.

In the second case the assertion is incomplete and inaccurate. This is because not only the right of nations to self-determination, but **all** the fundamental demands of political democracy are only partially "practicable" under imperialism, and then in a distorted form and by way of exception (for example, the secession of Norway from Sweden in 1905). The demand for the immediate liberation of the colonies that is put forward by all revolutionary Social-Democrats is also "impracticable" under capitalism without a series of revolutions. But from this it does not by any means follow that Social-Democracy should reject the immediate and most determined struggle for **all** these demands—such a rejection would only play into the hands of the bourgeoisie and reaction—but, on the contrary, it follows that these demands must be formulated and put through in a revolutionary and not a reformist manner, going beyond the bounds of bourgeois legality, breaking them down, going beyond speeches in parliament and verbal protests, and drawing the masses into decisive action, extending and intensifying the struggle for every fundamental democratic demand up to a direct proletarian onslaught on the bourgeoisie, i.e., up to the socialist revolution that expropriates the bourgeoisie. The socialist revolution may flare up not only through some big strike, street demonstration or hunger riot or a military insurrection or colonial revolt, but also as a result of a political crisis such as the Dreyfus[6] case or the Zabern[7] incident, or in connection with a referendum on the secession of an oppressed nation, etc.

Increased national oppression under imperialism does not mean that Social-Democracy should reject what the bourgeoisie call the "Utopian" struggle for the freedom of nations to secede but, on the contrary, it should make greater use of the conflicts that arise in this sphere, **too**, as grounds for mass action and for revolutionary attacks on the bourgeoisie.

Self-Determination and Its Relation to Federation

The right of nations to self-determination implies exclusively the right to independence in the political sense, the right to free political separation from the oppressor nation. Specifically, this demand for political democracy implies complete freedom to agitate for secession and for a referendum on secession by the seceding nation. This demand, therefore, is not the equivalent of a demand for separation, fragmentation and the formation of small states. It implies only a consistent expression of struggle against all national oppression. The closer a democratic state system is to complete freedom to secede the less frequent and less ardent will the desire for separation be in practice, because big states afford indisputable advantages, both from the standpoint of economic progress and from that of the interests of the masses and, furthermore, these advantages increase with the growth of capitalism. Recognition of self-determination is not synonymous with recognition of federation as a principle. One may be a determined opponent of that principle and a champion of democratic centralism but still prefer federation to national inequality as the only way to full democratic centralism. It was from this standpoint that Marx, who was a centralist, preferred even the federation of Ireland and England to the forcible subordination of Ireland to the English.

The aim of socialism is not only to end the division of mankind into tiny states and the isolation of nations in any form, it is not only to bring the nations closer together but to integrate them. And it is precisely in order to achieve this aim that we must, on the one hand, explain to the masses the reactionary nature of Renner's[8] and Otto Bauer's idea of so-called "cultural and national autonomy" and, on the other, demand the liberation of oppressed nations in a clearly and precisely formulated political programme that takes special account of the hypocrisy and cowardice of socialists in the oppressor nations, and not in general nebulous phrases, not in empty declamations and not by way of "relegating" the question until socialism has been achieved. In the same way as mankind can arrive at the abolition of classes only through a transition period of the dictatorship of the oppressed class, it can arrive at the inevitable integration of nations only through a transition period of the complete emancipation of all oppressed nations, i.e., their freedom to secede.

Proletarian-Revolutionary Presentation of the Question of the Self-Determination of Nations

The petty bourgeoisie had put forward not only the demand for the self-determination of nations but **all** the points

163

of our democratic minimum programme long before, as far back as the seventeenth and eighteenth centuries. They are still putting them all forward in a Utopian manner because they fail to see the class struggle and its increased intensity under democracy, and because they believe in "peaceful" capitalism. That is the exact nature of the utopia of a peaceful union of equal nations under imperialism which deceives the people and which is defended by Kautsky's followers. The programme of Social-Democracy, as a counter-balance to this petty-bourgeois, opportunist utopia, must postulate the division of nations into oppressor and oppressed as basic, significant and inevitable under imperialism.

The proletariat of the oppressor nations must not confine themselves to general, stereotyped phrases against annexation and in favour of the equality of nations in general, such as any pacifist bourgeois will repeat. The proletariat cannot remain silent on the question of the **frontiers** of a state founded on national oppression, a question so "unpleasant" for the imperialist bourgeoisie. The proletariat must struggle against the enforced retention of oppressed nations within the bounds of the given state, which means that they must fight for the right to self-determination. The proletariat must demand freedom of political separation for the colonies and nations oppressed by "their own" nation. Otherwise, the internationalism of the proletariat would be nothing but empty words; neither confidence nor class solidarity would be possible between the workers of the oppressed and the oppressor nations; the hypocrisy of the reformists and Kautskyites, who defend self-determination but remain silent about the nations oppressed by "their own" nation and kept in "their own" state by force, would remain unexposed.

On the other hand, the socialists of the oppressed nations must, in particular, defend and implement the full and unconditional unity, including organisational unity, of the workers of the oppressed nation and those of the oppressor nation. Without this it is impossible to defend the independent policy of the proletariat and their class solidarity with the proletariat of other countries in face of all manner of intrigues, treachery and trickery on the part of the bourgeoisie. The bourgeoisie of the oppressed nations persistently utilise the slogans of national liberation to deceive the workers; in their internal policy they use these slogans for reactionary agreements with the bourgeoisie of the dominant nation (for example, the Poles in Austria and Russia who come to terms with reactionaries for the oppression of the Jews and Ukrainians); in their foreign policy they strive to come to terms with one of the rival imperialist powers for the sake of implementing their predatory plans (the policy of the small Balkan states, etc.).

The fact that the struggle for national liberation against one imperialist power may, under certain conditions, be utilised by another "great" power for its own, equally imperialist, aims, is just as unlikely to make the Social-

Democrats refuse to recognise the right of nations to self-determination as the numerous cases of bourgeois utilisation of republican slogans for the purpose of political deception and financial plunder (as in the Romance countries, for example) are unlikely to make the Social-Democrats reject their republicanism.

Marxism and Proudhonism on the National Question

In contrast to the petty-bourgeois democrats, Marx regarded every democratic demand without exception not as an absolute, but as an historical expression of the struggle of the masses of the people, led by the bourgeoisie, against feudalism. There is not one of these demands which could not serve and has not served, under certain circumstances, as an instrument in the hands of the bourgeoisie for deceiving the workers. To single out, in this respect, one of the demands of political democracy, specifically, the self-determination of nations, and to oppose it to the rest, is fundamentally wrong in theory. In practice, the proletariat can retain its independence only by subordinating its struggle for all democratic demands, not excluding the demand for a republic, to its revolutionary struggle for the overthrow of the bourgeoisie.

On the other hand, in contrast to the Proudhonists[9] who "denied" the national problem "in the name of social revolution" Marx, mindful in the first place of the interests of the proletarian class struggle in the advanced countries, put the fundamental principle of internationalism and socialism in the foreground—namely, that no nation can be free if it oppresses other nations. It was from the standpoint of the interests of the German workers' revolutionary movement that Marx in 1848 demanded that victorious democracy in Germany should proclaim and grant freedom to the nations oppressed by the Germans. It was from the standpoint of the revolutionary struggle of the English workers that Marx, in 1869, demanded the separation of Ireland from England, and added: ". . .even if federation should follow upon separation." Only by putting forward this demand was Marx really educating the English workers in the spirit of internationalism. Only in this way could he counterpose the opportunists and bourgeois reformism —which even to this day, half a century later, has not carried out the Irish "reform"—with a revolutionary solution of the given historical task. Only in this way could Marx maintain—unlike the apologists of capital who shout that the freedom of small nations to secede is Utopian and impracticable and that not only economic but also political concentration is progressive — that this concentration is progressive when it is **non-imperialist**, and that nations should not be brought together by force, but by a free union of the proletarians of all countries. Only in this way could Marx, in opposition to the merely verbal, and often hypocritical, recognition of the equality and self-determination of nations, advocate the revolutionary action of the masses in the settlement of national questions **as well**. The imperialist war of 1914-16, and the Augean stables of hypocrisy on the part of the opportunists and Kautskyites that it has exposed, have strikingly confirmed the correctness of Marx's policy, which should serve as a model for all advanced countries, for all of them are now oppressing other nations.

Three Types of Countries with Respect to the Self-Determination of Nations

In this respect, countries must be divided into three main types. First, the advanced capitalist countries of Western Europe and the United States. In these countries progressive bourgeois national movements came to an end long ago. Every one of these "great" nations oppresses other nations both in the colonies and at home. The tasks of the proletariat of these ruling nations are the same as those of the proletariat in England in the nineteenth century in relation to Ireland.

Secondly, Eastern Europe: Austria, the Balkans and particularly Russia. Here it was the twentieth century that particularly developed the bourgeois-democratic national movements and intensified the national struggle. The tasks of the proletariat in these countries both in completing their bourgeois-democratic reforms, and rendering assistance to the socialist revolution in other countries, cannot be carried out without championing the right of nations to self-determination. The most difficult and most important task in this is to unite the class struggle of the workers of the oppressor nations with that of the workers of the oppressed nations.

Thirdly, the semi-colonial countries, such as China, Persia and Turkey, and all the colonies, which have a combined population of 1,000 million. In these countries the bourgeois-democratic movements either have hardly begun, or have still a long way to go. Socialists must not only demand the unconditional and immediate liberation of the colonies without compensation—and this demand in its political expression signifies nothing else than the recognition of the right to self-determination; they must also render determined support to the more revolutionary elements in the bourgeois-democratic movements for national liberation in these countries and assist their uprising—or revolutionary war, in the event of one—*against* the imperialist powers that oppress them.

Social-Chauvinism and the Self-Determination of Nations

The imperialist epoch and the war of 1914-16 has laid special emphasis on the struggle against chauvinism and nationalism in the leading countries. There are two main trends on the self-determination of nations among the social-chauvinists, that is, among the opportunists and Kautskyites, who hide the imperialist, reactionary nature of the war by applying to it the "defence of the fatherland" concept.

On the one hand, we see quite undisguised servants of the bourgeoisie who defend annexation on the plea that imperialism and political concentration are progressive, and who deny what they call the Utopian, illusory, petty-bourgeois, etc., right to self-determination. This includes the extreme opportunists in Germany, some of the Fabians and trade union leaders in England, and the opportunists in Russia.

On the other hand, we see the Kautskyites, among whom are many pacifists in Britain and France, and others. They favour unity with the former and in practice are completely identified with them; they defend the right to self-determination hypocritically and by words alone: they consider "excessive" ("**zu viel verlangt**": Kautsky in *Die Neue Zeit*, May 21, 1915) the demand for free political separation, they do not defend the necessity for revolutionary tactics on the part of the socialists of the oppressor nations in particular but, on the contrary, obscure their revolutionary obligations, justify their opportunism, make easy for them their deception of the people, and avoid the very question of the **frontiers** of a state forcefully retaining underprivileged nations within its bounds, etc.

Both are equally opportunist, they prostitute Marxism, having lost all ability to understand the theoretical significance and practical urgency of the tactics which Marx explained with Ireland as an example.

As for annexations, the question has become particularly urgent in connection with the war. But what is annexation? It is quite easy to see that a protest against

170

annexations either boils down to recognition of the self-determination of nations or is based on the pacifist phrase that defends the status quo and is hostile to **any**, even revolutionary, violence. Such a phrase is fundamentally false and incompatible with Marxism.

The Concrete Tasks of the Proletariat in the Immediate Future

The socialist revolution may begin in the very near future. In this case the proletariat will be faced with the immediate task of winning power, expropriating the banks and effecting other measures. The bourgeoisie—and especially the intellectuals of the Fabian and Kautskyite type— will, at such a moment, strive to split and check the revolution by foisting limited, democratic aims on it. Whereas **any** purely democratic demands are in a certain sense liable to act as a hindrance to the revolution, provided the proletarian attack on the pillars of bourgeois power has begun, the necessity to proclaim and grant liberty to **all** oppressed peoples (i.e., their right to self-determination) will be as urgent in the socialist revolution as it was for the victory of the bourgeois-democratic revolution in, say, Germany in 1848, or Russia in 1905.

It is possible, however, that years will elapse before the socialist revolution begins. This will be the time for the revolutionary education of the masses in a spirit that will make it impossible for socialist-chauvinists and opportunists to belong to the working-class party and gain a victory, as was the case in 1914-16. The socialists must explain to the masses that British socialists who do not demand freedom to separate for the colonies and Ireland, German socialists who do not demand freedom to separate for the colonies, the Alsatians, Danes and Poles, and who do not extend their revolutionary propaganda and revolutionary mass activity directly to the sphere of struggle against national oppression, or who do not make use of such incidents as that at Zabern for the broadest illegal propaganda among the proletariat of the oppressor nation, for street demonstrations and revolutionary mass action, Russian socialists who do not demand freedom to separate for Finland, Poland, the Ukraine, etc., etc.—that such socialists act as chauvinists and lackeys of bloodstained and filthy imperialist monarchies and the imperialist bourgeoisie.

Historical Specifics

If we look back on the dynamics of the dialectics between "our Rosa" and Comrade Illych - with the hindsight knowledge of the equivalent discourse as conducted between Dr. Newton and Prof. Erikson half a century later - it is clear that the argument has, in a sense, turned through a mirror. While Lenin's insight focused on a quest for the **logical definition** of a valid human collective, Newton reflected the tensions and contradictions on a more 'progressive' level, a more spiritual level: the level of collective **identity**. Newton's approach makes it impossible to avoid considering the implications of Revolutionary Intercommunalism for the individual consciousness[10]. In this sense Newton's position is the antithesis of Lenin's, reflecting as it does the existential morality, that is, personal responsibility, shouldered by the New Left[11].

More than thirty years after the Yale and Oakland meetings we can turn the dialectic through another mirror in search of a synthesis. But the image will not revert to anything comprehensible to a Bolshevik. Of course this is partly because of the rise and fall of the Soviet Union, and the coming to fruition of the economic and military hegemony of supranational corporations owned and controlled by hereditary dynasties. These dynasties have become feudal powers of global reach. They have no feudal sense of obligation to the people, whose labour and natural resources they exploit, but they enjoy overwhelming technological might (courtesy of the military and domestic control apparatuses of certain national states).

There is a second dimension of difference between the start of this century and the start of the last. It is the transformation in consciousness that has taken place across almost the entire planet because of the global media. To be historically specific this translates into mid-Wales in the midsummer of 2004 as a situation in which Big Brother vies with the football for space on the front page of the newspapers, but the TV schedules are able to accommodate both. This is not the Big Brother[12] smiling with approval at Home Secretary Blunkett's "prison without bars"; it is not the one raising his eyebrows as the Head of the CIA sees fit to resign after letting the cat out of the bag about proactive "Public Diplomacy"[13]; nor is it the one immortalised in the subtle, informal British equivalent of the US Patriot Act. No. This Big Brother is even more debilitating to the development of a responsible collective identity - it is **only** a TV show!

All this spooky surrealism in itself reflects a third level of paradigm shift: from Lenin's formulation of the collective **entity** and its appropriate methodology, through Newton's elucidation of the collective **identity** and its responsibilities, to the historical specifics of today's almost hopelessly **individualised** self-seeking identities and their relationships to

174

any possibility of a resurgence of internationalism, or revolutionary love.

My own individual historical identity is therefore a reference point for my attempt to bring this dialectic into a Here and Now. I am (to use a category conceived by the market research industry in answer to a question that governments did not trust sociologists to handle) "mixed race". But aren't we all? In my case it means I have North African features and what is, to my taste, far too light a touch of what the Brits used to call "the tar brush".

I am female. Again this puts me in the majority, nothing singular about that.

I am a displaced victim/beneficiary of the British empire. No prizes for originality here either. At different times in my family history I could have been born in Africa, India, Cornwall, Rome, The Lebanon, Romania, Yugoslavia, Egypt. In fact I was conceived on board ship in the Suez canal and born in England.

I am a Welsh citizen now. Warmly adopted by this well-favoured corner of the old Empire it is easy to get into feeling nationalistic. My lazy summer afternoon fantasy is of a deep, wide ditch dug across the border from sea to sea. Then we all dress up in the national costume with the tall hat, like for the tourists (only now the kids are confusing the gear with what you get from amazon.co.uk for Halloween), and we line up along the ditch with long pikes and just push off. So we can float Wales a little way out into the Irish Sea. Thus in NIMBY-ish imagination I can physically dissociate our majestic mountains and green valleys, our history of Chartism, socialism, Trades Unions, Cooperatives and resurgent Credit Unions, our principled self-sacrificing energy policy, our minstrels and bards; I can separate our lovely land from the encroaching motorways, from the MATRIX, the GPS and GALILEO technology, the mobile phone masts, MacDonald's, IKEA, genetically modified crops, precocious commercialised exploitative sexuality, Seroxat, Special Brew and "reality TV".

But this is infantile?

No it is **senile** - just as senile and degenerate as the petrol and Viagra fuelled, prosthetic-dependent, global mass culture to which it is a petty bourgeois reaction.

Jamaica is a land of similar size to Wales, equally a land of fantastic beauty, of mountains and music and poetry. The sea actually **does** go right around it. But it is obvious to anyone with the most cursory knowledge of the historical specifics that the sea has been no protection from exploitation, particularly by the British and American imperial dynasties. Slaves and sugar, coffee and guns can travel across the sea; cocaine and more guns can fly through the air; dollars and propaganda can be propelled by wire, radio or satellite

176

transmission. No island is an island.

Before a simplified, Bowdlerized form of Jamaican patois became the basis of commercialised adolescent street cool (via the ghettos of American and British inner cities and the video-game and popular music industries) the impenetrability of the patois was a better defence than any physical barrier. In its arcane and yet highly dynamic localised dialects it still is. It is a code that simply cannot be cracked by an artificial intelligence. Foreign intelligence and crime control agencies need a lot of time and patience (a high degree of effective HUMINT[14] penetration) to master it, just as has been the case throughout Africa, Asia and the Middle East. They will not succeed without some covert dealings with the local power structures[15].

Suffice it to say that the Welsh have a language too! It is this and not the sea which affords them their best hope against exploitation.

Though nationalism must never become the end of our struggle against those who want to burn up the whole earth, it is undeniably the beginning. It is simply Common Sense[16] that nationalism may often be the historically appropriate first stage of political awakening for the dispossessed. Parties such as the Black Panthers, Plaid Cymru and the New Jewel Movement set a precedent for the Internationalist maxim, **"Think Global: Act Local"**, a maxim which is the quintessence of the Kantian categorical imperative. Their nationalism (unlike that of, say, the British National Party or the UK Independence Party) is premised on the ultimate goal of internationalism.

I vote for the Plaid, support the Welsh Assembly, and campaign for a proper independent tax-levying and law-making body. I vote for a Plaid Cymru MEP in the European parliament as well as for a representative in the Assembly. But as a British citizen I also treasure the right to vote for an MP in Westminster and I honour the memory of the Chartists and Suffragettes whose struggle secured that vote for me. I will brandish my British rights in the face of the oppressors of our people, just as Huey Newton brandished his American right to carry a firearm.

As a British citizen I treasure all the rights that the people of these lands have had to fight for, the trades unions, the independent system of justice, the "Nanny State" (with its free schools and hospitals and welfare cushions against poverty, unemployment, sickness, disability and old age); most of all I treasure the possibility of "Speaking Truth to Power". But I am very well aware of the degree to which, in the last few decades, these specific historical compensations have been undermined and eroded as opportunistic (and sometimes heinous) governance has aided and abetted the rise of the shadowy supranational pirates.

The most disastrous mistake in the history of the

United Kingdom was made in the 1960s - just at the very time when a new generation of the common people was growing up less scarred by war , ignorance, poverty and disease than any before it. The mistake was to sacrifice the most precious asset "Britain" ever had - the fruits of its ill-gotten empire - in pursuit of two mutually antagonistic and highly damaging objectives:

1. Atlanticism
2. The European Common Market

The painstaking and life-costly business of transforming the pink-coloured parts of the world map from "British Empire" to "Commonwealth of Nations" was almost complete as the government in Westminster achieved a measure of success in curtailing the power of the robber barons and (not before time) conceding independence, nation by nation.

The Commonwealth was set to become just that, a **common-wealth.** Left to its own logic it would have matured as a massive international political and economic entity, enjoying access to every conceivable natural resource and untold potential material wealth, which would have been expropriated by the heirs of the exploited from the heirs of the exploiters without further bloodshed. This commonwealth would have had recourse to talents and skills of staggering diversity. There would have been a dynamic interaction

179

between ancient and venerable cultures and fast-changing peripatetic groupings sparkling with cosmopolitan and bohemian originality. It would have been blessed with the moral authority of political and ethical giants from Gandichi to Mandiba.

All that was needed was one simple Common Sense transformation of definition: Britain simply had to become one equal member of the Commonwealth. This would have required a fairly small adjustment to the constitutional definition of an international body which at that time was still based on the essential universalistic principles of Separation of Powers, *Habeas Corpus,* universal literacy and participative democracy. If it had gone on to create a new international Commonwealth court of justice to replace the House of Lords as arbiter of final resort, such a Commonwealth could even have afforded to allow the British monarch to hang on to the figure-head role for another generation.

My own view is that this not only **could** have been achieved, but that the economic and political trajectories of the world as a whole were such that it **would actually have happened** if "a small group of politically motivated men" had not set out to prevent it.

Let me make this quite unambiguous. I am saying that the internal logic of the mid-twentieth century post-imperial enlightenment expressed the will of the people of the British

Commonwealth towards a non-violent revolutionary intercommunal grouping - a genuinely political amalgamation of bottom-up democratic mechanisms of governance.

The material advantages for all parties would have been obvious. And the cultural prerequisites were already in place in the early 1960s when students of imperial history like myself could share a desk with the Grenadian High Commissioner in the British Library and then leg it over to the Commonwealth Institute for a quick curry with Julius Nyrere. Given all the education and good will and respectful non-violent revolutionary consciousness of those times it is clear that reactionary atavism would have needed actual conspiracy to abort the coming internationalism. Actually of course there were two (diametrically opposed) conspiracy groupings which succeeded very effectively in emasculating the progressive potential of the Commonwealth and advancing the cause of the very dynasties who are today Hell-bent on destroying our planet for their own short-term gain: they can be nailed with the tags of Atlanticism on the one hand and Europeanism on the other.

The concepts of **Revolutionary Intercommunalism** and **Self-Determination** explained by Newton and Lenin in this volume make it clear that a dialectical understanding is one that recognises that what may be the best move in one place at one time could be the wrong move in a different place or time. I believe that Britain should never have "gone into"

Europe. But this does not mean that Welsh peasants like myself should be supporting the right-wing political parties who want to get out of the European Union now. For one thing, we may sometimes need to brandish our European rights in the face of our home-grown authoritarian government![17] Understanding the contradictions in capitalism is vital to navigating a route across the minefield that the expropriators have made of our world. Whether we like it or not we are all affected by international groupings such as the UN, CIS, EEC, OPEC, ASEAN, G8 and NATO etc., some of which include us and some of which exclude us. At every point in time and space we need to recalculate our position with regard to these acronymous entities, to the nation states which comprise or oppose them, and to the local communities in whose particularistic conditions we have to work out our universalism.

Notes

1. The opportunists to whom Lenin refers are Semkovsky, "The Russian Liquidator" (who called upon the workers to cease their revolutionary struggle against tsarism and sought to create a legal opportunist organisation engaged only in activity permitted by the tsarist government), Liebman the Bundist (see note 5 below) and the Ukranian National Socialist, Yurkevich (who was an active contributor to the Menshevik-inclined nationalist journal *Dzvin* (The Bell). Lenin regarded him as a philistine and representative of the basest most reactionary nationalism.

2. The Editor of the 1947 Progress Edition of Lenin's *The Right of Nations to Self-Determination* indexed Kautsky thus:

KAUTSKY, KARL (1854-1938) – leader of German Social Democracy and the Second International; first a Marxist and later a renegade and ideologist of the most dangerous and pernicious variety of opportunism, Centrism, i.e. social chavinism cloaked in internationalist phraseology; editor of the theoretical journal of German Social Democracy , *Die Neue Zeit*.

3. BAUER, OTTO (1882-1938)— one of the leaders of the Austrian Social-Democratic Party and the Second International, ideologist of so-called "Austro-Marxism", a variety of reformism. He was one of the authors of the bourgeois-nationalist theory of "cultural-national autonomy", the opportunistic nature of which was repeatedly exposed by Lenin. Bauer adopted a negative attitude towards the October Socialist Revolution; from 1918 to 1919 he was Minister for Foreign Affairs of the Austrian Republic and actively participated in crushing the revolutionary actions of the Austrian working class.

4. LASSALLE, FERDINAND (1825-1864) – a founder of the General Association of German Workers, which though initially a benefit for the working class movement was led during Lassalle's presidency along a petty bourgeois opportunist path which was sharply criticized by both Marx and Engels.

5. The Bund was the General Jewish Workers' Union of Lithuania, Poland and Russia, which was organised in 1897 and was mainly an association of Jewish artisans living in the western regions of Russia. The Bund was affiliated to the Russian Social-Democratic Labour Party (R.S.D.L.P) at the latter's First Congress in March 1898. At the Second Congress of the R.S.D.L.P. held between July 17 and August 10 , 1903 the Bundists demanded that the Bund be recognised as the sole representative of the Jewish proletariat; the Congress rejected this organisational nationalism of the Bund, and the latter left the Party.

After the Fourth (Unity) Congress in 1906 the Bund again entered the R.S.D.L.P. Its members gave constant support to the Mensheviks and fought against the Bolsheviks. Although it belonged, formally, to the R.S.D.L.P., the Bund was a bourgeois nationalist organisation. It put forward the demand for cultural-national autonomy in opposition to the Bolsheviks' programme demand for the right of nations to self-determination. The Bund played an active part in the formation of the August anti-Party bloc. At the Prague Conference of the R.S.D.L.P., in January 1912, its members were expelled from the Party together with other opportunists. During the First World War the Bund members adopted the position of social- chauvinism; in 1917 the Bund supported the bourgeois Provisional Government and fought on the side of the enemies of the October Socialist Revolution. During the Civil War leading Bundists joined ranks with the counter-revolutionary forces. At the same time there was a change taking place among rank-and-file members of the Bund who began to favour collaboration with Soviet power. When the victory of the proletarian dictatorship over the internal counter-revolution and foreign intervention became obvious the Bund declared that it would renounce its struggle against Soviet power. In March 1921 the Bund announced its dis-solution and part of its membership entered the Russian Communist Party (Bolsheviks).

6. The Dreyfus Case was a provocative trial instituted in 1894 by reactionary royalist circles among the French militarists against the Jewish General Staff officer Dreyfus who was falsely accused of espionage and high treason. A court martial condemned Dreyfus to life imprisonment. The public movement for a re-examination of the Dreyfus case that developed in France took the form of a fierce struggle between the republicans and the royalists and led to the eventual release of Dreyfus in 1906. Lenin called the Dreyfus case "one of the many thousands of fraudulent tricks of the reactionary military clique",

7. The incident took place in the town of Zabern (Alsace) in November 1913. It was caused by the brutality of a Prussian officer towards the Alsatians. It gave rise to an outburst of indignation among the local, mainly French, population, directed against the Prussian militarists. (See Lenin's article "Zabern" in *Collected Works,* Vol. 19, pp. 513-15.

8. Lenin criticised the reactionary idea of "cultural-national autonomy", advanced by Renner and Bauer, in an article entitled "Cultural-National Autonomy" *(Collected Works,* Vol. 19, pp. 503-07) and in his "Critical Remarks on the National Question" *(Collected Works,* Vol. 20, pp. 17-51.

9. PROUDHON, PIERRE-JOSEPH (1809-1865) - French publicist, economist and sociologist, petty-bourgeois ideologist and one of the founders of anarchism; he advocated small-scale private property and criticised large-scale capitalist property from petty-bourgeois positions. He considered the state to be the principal source of class contradictions and put forward Utopian projects for "eliminating the state" peacefully, opposing all forms of political struggle. Proudhon and his followers held idiosyncratic views on - the national question, asserting that the concepts of nationality and nation were "outdated prejudices", and opposed the national liberation movements of the oppressed nations. In his *Poverty of Philosophy* and other works Marx sharply criticised the theory

186

and political positions of Proudhonism and exposed their anti-scientific and reactionary nature.

10. See H P Newton *To Die for the People* (Writers and Readers,1995) and Frederika Newton and David Hilliard *War Against the Panthers* (Writers and Readers,2001).

11. George Lukacs was prominent among these thinkers who were also influenced by the publication of Marx's 1844 "manuscripts" in English translation. Consult bibliography below.

12. Until the term was associated in the public consciousness with a TV programme it was understood, since George Orwell's novel *1984*, to mean something akin to Bentham's panopticon. See Semple (Clarendon,1993).

13. This was on BBC Radio 4 in May 2004. The previous year Lieutenant-Colonel Steven Collins (head of PSYOPS at NATO Supreme HQ in Mons, Belgium) bragged on the NATO website (www.nato.int/docu/review/2003/english/art4.htmlxt) that "Perception management includes all actions used to influence the attitudes and objective reasoning of foreign audiences and consists of Public Diplomacy, Psychological Operations (PSYOPS), Public Information, Deception and Covert Action". Cited in *Lobster*, Vol 46, 2003, p.14. See also Frances Stonor Saunders, *Who Paid the Piper* (Granta,1999).

14. HUMINT is long established security jargon for human intelligence, as opposed to electronic surveillance , or SIGINT.

15. For a dangerously precise exposition of the relationship between the dons and organised crime in the United States see

Laurie Gunst, *Born Fi Dead: A Journey through the yardie underworld* (Payback,2003).

16. See Tom Paine's essay on Common Sense where the same dialectic is examined in the context of American Independence.

17. A horrible frissant of this was experienced in Wales during the outbreak of the "Foot and Mouth" virus in 2001 when commercial interests colluded with an authoritarian government in a mass slaughter of healthy livestock burned in stinking pyres throughout our land. While commerical meat farmers, and a variety of other opportunists made a packet by manipulating the subsidies (and other dodges) the ordinary peasants were unable to save their flocks from the slaughter squads. Activists and protestors soon found themselves targets of unusual measures, many of us suspecting, as later uncovered by David Miller, that we were guinea pigs in a newly ratcheted-up internal propaganda system for dealing with national "emergencies". See Miller (Pluto,2004) p.85.

BIBLIOGRAPHY

AQUINAS, St. Thomas, *Selected Philosophical Writings*
(Oxford World's Classics, 1998)

AYER, A.J., *Language Truth and Logic* (Peter Smith Pub.,1952)

BOX, Steven, *Deviance Reality and Society* (Holt R & W, 1971)

CHOMSKY, Noam, *Hegemony or Survival* (Penguin,2004)

CONFUCIUS,*The Analects* (Oxford World's Classics,2000)

DOUGLASS, Frederick, *Narrative of the life of Frederick
Douglass, an American Slave*(DoverThrift,1995)

ERIKSON, Kai T., *Wayward Puritans* (Macmillan, 1968)

ERIKSON, E H and NEWTON, H P *In Search of Common
Ground* (Laurel,1974)

FOUCAULT, Michel, *The Order of Things* (Routledge, 2001)

FUKUYAMA, F., *The End of History and the Last Man*
(Penguin,1993)

GUNST, Laurie, *Born Fi Dead* (Payback Press, 2003)

HARDT, M and NEGRI, A, *(Empire,* Harvard U P, 2001)

HOBBES, Thomas, *Leviathan* (Oxford World's Classics, 1998)

KANT, Immanuel, *Critique of Pure Reason* {abridged}
(Hackett, 1999)

KIERKEGAARD, Soren, *The Essential Kierkegaard* (Princeton
University Press, 2000)

LENIN, Vladimir I, *Collected Works,* Volumes *19-22* (Progress,
Moscow,1947)

LUKACS, Georg, *The Lukacs Reader,* (Blackwell, 1995).

LUXEMBURG, Rosa, *Reform or Revolution* (Pathfinder,1973)

MARX, Karl, *Capital* (Penguin, 1992)

The Manuscripts of 1844, Ed. by Struik (International, 1964)

MILLER, David (Ed) *Tell me Lies* (Pluto,2004)

MILLS, C Wright, *Sociological Imagination* (Oxford U.P., 2000)

NEWTON, Huey P, *Revolutionary Suicide* (Writers and Readers, 1995);

To Die for the People, Ed. Morrison (Writers and Readers, 1995);

and NEWTON, Frederika, *War Against the Panthers* (Writers and Readers, 2001)

ORWELL, George, *Nineteen Eighty-Four* (Penguin,1981)

PAINE, Thomas, *Common Sense* (Dover, Thrift,1997)

PILGER, John, *The New Rulers of the World* (Verso,2003)

PLATO, *The Republic* (Cambridge U.P., 2000)

SAUNDERS, Frances S, *Who Paid the Piper* (Granta, 1999)

SEMPLE, Janet, *Bentham's Prison* (Clarenden, 1993)

TODD, Paul and BLOCH, Jonathan, *Global Intelligence* (Zed Books, 2003)

TRESSELL, Robert, *The Ragged Trousered Philanthropists* (Flamingo,1991)

VENTOUR, John et al, *In the Spirit of Butler* (Fedon,1982)

ZOLA, Emile, *Germinal* (Oxford World's Classics,1998)

"...we have every opportunity and every encouragement before us, to form the noblest, purest constitution on the face of the earth. We have it in our power to begin the world over again."

Thomas Paine, *Common Sense*

For your notes:-

• downfall of BPP, done in a subtle way so as to
avert attention away from FBI and the govt.
Clear to many of the public that Newton and the
BPP brought it upon themselves.

• Reform comes through 'education' in a subject
in the sense of heightening the collective conscience
of masses. Of course not everyone will be converted to the
ways of accepting blacks immediately, but many will be. Dee
not need the revolutionary socialist tag in that this expansio
of individuals conscious can be achieved under capitalism.
This is if whites see a few black power that is representative
of what is expected in a human being, and individuals
such as Huey Newton and S Carmichael are perfect
candidates for that as they have the good of the
masses in mind. Preconceptions of black people shattered
by key figures of this time, educated everyone. Of
course contradiction comes in the form of having to
almost such up to whites and give in to what Fanon
claimed was a natural urge, to kill your oppressor.
Not all white men oppressors of course, recognised
clearly by BPP with Newton seeing them as part of
the same struggle, the struggle that everyone willing
needed to be involved in.

192